T0149872

EMBRACING THE WORLD

Fethullah Gülen's Thought and
Its Relationship to Jalaluddin Rumi and Others

EMBRACING THE WORLD

Fethullah Gülen's Thought and
Its Relationship to Jalaluddin Rumi and Others

Ori Z. Soltes

TUGHRA
BOOKS

New Jersey

Published by Tughra Books
345 Clifton Ave., Clifton,
NJ, 07011, USA

www.tughrabooks.com

Library of Congress Cataloging-in-Publication Data Available

ISBN: 978-1-59784-288-4

Printed by
Imak Ofset, Istanbul - Turkey

Contents

For Ali Yurtsever, Ermal Hitaj and Jena Luedtke:
friends, models, bearers of that inimitable Light.

"Miracles don't cause faith, but rather
the scent of kindredness that unites people...

...Everyone understands this voice when it comes.
It speaks with the same authority to Turk and Kurd,
Persian, Arab, Ethiopian, [Albanian, American,] one language!"

—Jalaluddin Rumi

Preface

This is neither a comprehensive study of Fethullah Gülen nor a comprehensive study of Jalaluddin Rumi. What I am seeking to do is to explore the places where the thought of the one is echoed in the thinking of the other, either overtly or indirectly—and to note ways in which the opposite is true: that Gülen diverges from Rumi.

I am also seeking to suggest some of the larger contexts in which the thinking of both resides. Given the wide-ranging aspects of their respective writings, it should not be surprising if, minimally, we can find important foundation stones in both philosophy and theology in the edifices that they each construct. Given the important role of Muslim thinkers in the era leading to and beyond the time of Rumi in preserving and transmitting the thought of the ancient Greeks, it should not be surprising to find traces of Plato in Rumi, together with important influences from prior Muslim and in particular prior Sufi thinkers. Given Gülen's wide interests it should not be surprising to find echoes from the same array of thinkers that have come both through his own study of them and through his engagement of Rumi.

Moreover, Gülen's intellectual interests extend beyond the era of Rumi, and thus others—notably Bediüzzaman Said Nursi—have added to the foundations of his edifice of thought. And in the long run, this narrative evolves primarily as a focus on Fethullah Gülen as one, inspired by Rumi and others, who is a scholar of Islam who has transformed the theory of universalism into a concerted and successful plan of action on various levels.

Gülen has spent most of his life as a student of the Qur'an and of Islamic literature and lore and a good part of that time as an avid learner—like the Prophet Muhammad himself seems, by every account, to have been—of a wide range of subjects, spiritual and otherwise. He has evolved the sort of philosophy that offers a unique form of hope and potential help for a world fraught with fractiousness and contention, where greed seems to be a defining attribute of those in power and desperation of those without power.

Gülen's vision is Islamist—in two ways: he speaks from within the deepest reaches of his own Muslim traditions, and his vision for his own country, Turkey, is that it reclaim the Muslim identity that is endemic to the last nearly thousand years of its history and to its national soul. At the same time, he is emphatically universalist: his vision is one in which each country addresses the world from within the traditions that have shaped its national soul, but all countries ultimately share a common goal: to improve the world for all humans and also for the non-human elements that make up the world.

He has articulated his vision in terms of an altruistic sensibility. This is the opposite of the "me" emphasis that has been expressed by various writers and pundits in the course of history and in particular the twentieth and early twenty-first centuries. And he has pushed the growing cadre of adherents to his banner to translate the theory that he espouses into action: service to the community and ultimately the world around them. He has taught and preached and written about universal love and compassion, not only for fellow humans, but for the natural world around us.

As a practicing Sufi—an adherent of Muslim mysticism—Gülen is comfortable with paradox and has shaped his thinking in accordance with the paradoxes that are inherent in mysticism. God is within us and God is unimaginably beyond us. God is inaccessible, yet the hiddenmost recesses of God are accessible. As the mystic seeks God, God seeks the mystic. We must seek God from deep within our own tradition; there are myriad traditions from which paths lead to the same inner recess of God: the *mysterion*.

This is a perspective to which many mystics have arrived—and I spend a considerable amount of time in the introductory and first chapters exploring this in order to provide a solid foundation upon which readers, particularly those new to this area of spirituality, may build the edifice of their understanding. But none has articulated the idea as frequently or as lyrically as did the thirteenth-century Sufi, Jalaluddin Rumi. Thus there is a range of distinct connections that may be found between Rumi in his time and Gülen in his time—our time. Fundamentally, the one spoke and taught and wrote and the other speaks and teaches and writes of issues that reach beyond themselves because they are not time-bound.

Ultimately a central point of this discussion is to demonstrate how (without presuming to state definitively as to why), within broad intellectual, cultural and spiritual frameworks, two individuals so far *apart* in time can be and have been within their respective times of thinking, feeling and writing, *ahead* of their time—and ultimately timeless, at least to those willing to listen carefully to their respective words.

Or as Rumi put it:

> I am so small I can barely be seen.
> How can this great love be inside me?
>
> *Look at your eyes.*
> *They are small, but they see enormous things.*
> *(Divani Shamsi Tabriz #798)*

The great love is the love of God and the love of all of God's creation. The eyes with which he sees so much are not merely those with which we see the outside world and the outer shapes of things, but those with which we see both within and beyond. Rumi was talking to himself, but also, one might say, to Fethullah Gülen—as Gülen himself may be seen to recognize, when he writes (in the foreword to Shefik Can's book on Rumi), that the thirteenth-century Sufi master "hastened toward God on his own spiritual journey, but in addition to this he evoked similar journeys in countless others—journeys marked by an eager striving toward God."[1]

Gülen clearly includes himself among those countless others— which is why he wrote the foreword to Can's book, with such obvi-

---

[1] M. Fethullah Gülen, "Foreword" in Shefik Can: *Fundamentals of Rumi's Thought: A Mevlevi Sufi Perspective*, Somerset, NJ: Tughra Books, 2008.

ous love and eagerness, in the first place. But Rumi's words, as Gülen recognizes, are really directed to all humans who share the potential to hear and see and who value and seek to hear and see inwardly as much as and sometimes more than outwardly. This is a sentiment shared, in fact, by Rumi and Gülen, each of whom in his own way is an important part of exploring and explaining how to carry "this great love ... inside me" out to the world.

With this last comment in mind I wish to offer my gratitude to two individuals in particular whose interest led to the bringing of this book to fruition: Ali Yurtsever, former Director of the Rumi Forum in Washington, DC who suggested it; and Emre Celik, current Director, whose constant attention led to its completion and arrival at the publishing house. I would also like to thank the editors at Tughra Press for their careful attention to every detail within my text, and for their patience and generosity of spirit. Teşekkür!

Introduction

J alaluddin Rumi, as we shall soon see in some detail, is the founder of a particular *tariqa*—a particular group with its particular sensibilities—within the diverse history of Muslim mysticism. As this book focuses most directly (but not exclusively) on his putative influence on the contemporary social and political philosopher-theologian, Fethullah Gülen, then one of the starting points of this narrative is to consider what mysticism is, in order to try to understand how it shapes and is shaped by the thought of someone like Rumi and why and how such thought should end up affecting the thinking and writing of someone like Gülen.

Religion: The Realm of the *Sacer*

An understanding of mysticism requires a grasp of the broad purposes of religion. Religion presupposes an opposition between the life of the everyday, the safely circumscribed, the familiar and knowable, the human—and a realm beyond the human: unknown and ultimately, in a most fundamental sense, unknowable, fraught with both hope and fear, with both positive and negative possibilities. That realm, so rigorously separated from the realm of the day-to-day is referred to in English as the "sacred."

It might be useful for our purposes to use the Latin term upon which the English word is based—*sacer*—since the latter accomplishes three things that the former generally does not. First, and perhaps most importantly, "*sacer*" is not readily familiar to most of us the way "sacred" is, so encountering it in a text forces us to stop short and ask what it means, rather than automatically assuming that we already know that term and gliding by it without much thought.

Second, the Latin term has a wider range of aspectual meanings than the English term has come to possess. It encompasses the unknown in all of its aspects, and refers to any reality that operates according to principles in time and space that have an irrational, illogical or unintelligible quality to them. Thus the wilderness, the desert, the high seas, outer space, on the one hand; and on the other, the realm of sleep and dreams and the realm of death are all aspects of the *sacer*, as well as the realm of divinity.

These sub-aspects of the concept share the quality of being unpredictable, and of not operating in time and space according to our expectations. Dreams notoriously bounce from one time or space frame to another in a manner analogous to the way in which we understand divinity to perceive all of time and space as a coherent, present-tense continuum within God's purview. For humans, when we are awake, time and space offer a linear way of being, past leads to present which leads to future and the distance between Washington, DC and New York is understandably different from that between Washington and Istanbul.

This second feature of the *sacer* interweaves the third: that it is inherently neutral in its disposition to us, and potentially positive or negative. Thus in the wild woods nothing may occur to us, or wolves may devour us, or our fairy god mother may tap us on the shoulder and give us three wonderful wishes that change our life. When we sleep, we may have no dreams or sweet dreams or nightmares. When we die, perhaps nothing happens to us, or perhaps we go to a wonderful place (call it Paradise) or perhaps to a terrible place (call it the Inferno). When we seek the gods or God, we may receive no response, or a negative response or a positive response: praying for rain may yield further draught or a flood or just the right amount of rain to offer us continued life.

The boundless *sacer*, in its aspect as divinity, may, in most religious traditions, assume myriad shapes (or none at all): gods and goddesses, *daimons* and spirits, sometimes benevolent and sometimes malicious, unpredictable and intrinsically inaccessible to the modes of access with which humans ordinarily address the world around us: the five senses and the intellect.

The term *sacer* can also apply to an individual, in which case it also implies being apart from the community, the familiar, the everyday: so (in the positive sense) a prophet or priest is one separate from the community, particularly, in the case of a priest, in the enactment of rituals. Such a figure, in turn, guides the community (the *profanus*) in its relationship with the *sacer;* hence that figure is termed, in Latin, *sacerdos*—"one who gives the *sacer* [to us]," (and "one who gives us to the *sacer*").[2] So, too, (in the negative sense), one who has transgressed a *boundary* between *profanus* and *sacer* space, becomes, as we shall see, *sacer*.

It is the province and purpose of religion to wrestle with all of this. Thus religion not only *addresses* that realm beyond the everyday, but defines how we should *understand* it. The word "religion" itself indicates this. It is a straightforward development of the Latin word *religio*, the root of which—"-lig-"—means a "binding" (one finds that root in "lig-aments," that bind muscle to bone, and "lig-atures," that bind up wounds, for example). *Religio* binds a community together with regard to its sense of the *sacer*. More precisely, since *"re-"* means "back" or "again," religion binds a community *back again* to that aspect of the *sacer* realm—divinity—which it assumes *created* it.

Religion prescribes the times and spaces within which, addressing the *sacer*, we make it more accessible to our aspirations. Religious rite and ritual govern the boundaries between ourselves and the *sacer*, regulating their traversal when appropriate, structuring the process with minutely detailed care in order to insure as much as possible a positive response from that realm toward our own realm. *Sacerdotes* are those who, in every religious tradition, are believed to possess the peculiar knowledge (granted to them in revelation from the *sacer*) of what rituals and rites to prescribe and of how properly to accomplish them. So, in their respective traditions: Abraham, Moses, Jesus, Muhammad, Bud-

---

2 A slightly different theory derives *sacerdos* from *sacer* + an Indo-European root **dhe*, meaning "do," thus: "do, make *sacer*."

dha, the Bab; the priest in the Israelite Temple, in the Sumerian Great
Ziqqurat, in the Temple to Jupiter Capitolinus in Rome.

Each religion assumes that the divine powers of the *sacer* are, on
the whole, beneficent (that assumption is present, both for Roman
polytheism and for the evolving Israelite-Judean monotheism that is
contemporary with it). So to be *sacer*—to be what the gods are, to be
with the gods—must mean to be *blessed*. Thus, for example, in dying,
one may come to reside with the gods—a blessed condition concerning which there is ample discussion in Greco-Roman and other
mythologies. Yet in the case of a *scapegoat*, that animal, *sacer*, is clearly
understood to be *cursed*. The bilateral, paradoxic nature of the *sacer*,
then, is clear—and is essential to Western religious history. For Christianity, Jesus as the ultimate sacerdotal being (he is both human and
divine for Christians) in earthly death, becomes *sacer*. In his death he
bears humanity's sins on his shoulders and thus, one might say, is as
cursed as one can be. But at the same time, he who returns to the
realm of God-the-Father is as blessed as one can possibly be.

In the Abrahamic traditions, it is through prophets and priests
(two separate but related modes of sacerdotal intermediation) that we
receive instruction from God as to how to be so that we may invite
blessing and not curse upon ourselves; and it is such individuals who
plead with God (the *sacer*) on our behalf. The Abrahamic traditions
share a plethora of prophetic figures in common and are distinguished
from each other in part by those they don't share—or concerning whom
they view their precise sacerdotal nature differently. Thus, for example, Jesus is one among many human prophets for Muslims. He is, more
precisely, one of the *Ulu al Azm*—the five most prominent prophets,
together with Noah, Abraham, Moses and Muhammad—but he is
unique, both human and divine, for Christians. (For Jews he is not a
prophet at all).

Religion and Mysticism: The *Mysterion* within the *Sacer*

Mysticism may be understood as a particularly intense aspect of religious experience—as a particular means of traversing the boundary
into relationship with the *sacer*. The term "mysticism," related to the

term "mystery," derives from the Latin *mysterium* which, in turn, derives from the Greek *mysterion*. This term, in turn, comes from the Greek verb *mystein*, meaning "to close" or, by extension, "to hide": the *mysterion* is the *closed*, the *hidden* center of the *sacer* which the mystic seeks to enter—and which the mystical method seeks to uncover.

That method (for which*ever* mystical system) is itself intrinsically hidden: the mystic hopes to travel hidden paths, to absorb hidden knowledge of interpreting and understanding the world by transcending its bounds into communion with the *sacer* that engendered our world. Mysticism presupposes that, within the heart of the *sacer*, deep-centered in its recesses, the hiddenness is the ultimate essence of the *sacer*—the ultimate goal of the ultimate hope of merging the mystic's *profanus* self with the *sacer*. That ultimate unknown is the wholly transcendent, wholly unintelligible, which is beyond "normative" religious ritual, to be sought by carefully and precisely prescribed methods inaccessible to "normative" religious method and sensibility.

Mysticism, moreover, implies a *personalized* communion with the *sacer*—as opposed to "normative" religious experience, with its strong communal emphasis, involving a *group* defined by its *religio* and mediated by its particular *sacerdotes* (this is the plural of *sacerdos*) and by its particular relationship to the *sacer*. Mystics who succeed, achieve ecstasy—*ek stasis* in Greek, meaning "out of [where one ordinarily] stands": they stand outside their normal, everyday state of being, in bursting the bounds of themselves via a method that carries them beyond normative patterns of logic and intuition. By further paradox, at least within the Abrahamic traditions, that *ek-stasis* may also be understood as *en-stasis*, since to find the hidden innermost recess of God one might dig into the innermost recesses of one's own soul, which is that aspect of God *within* all of us. Of course, when one deals with the *sacer*, one does not deal with the linear sort of space with which we are familiar in the everyday world, so looking inward as a means of looking outward has its own paradoxic *sacer* "spatial" logic.

The mystic must, if s/he would merge with the center of the *sacer*, be in perfect equilibrium within him/herself—centered, as the cosmos is, a pivot that spins without wobbling—so that, traveling beyond (or deeply within) his/her *profanus* self, s/he is able to return to that self without being harmed by the experience. Indeed, one of the important features of mysticism in the Abrahamic traditions is the obligation of the mystic to *return* to the world of the here and now and to benefit the community of which s/he remains a part, with whatever insights have been gained through communion with the innermost recesses of the unknown. So the *real* goal is not to *enter* the hiddenmost recesses of the *sacer*, but to get there and *return* to the everyday world and to the community within it, changed, bettered, and in a position to change and improve the world of which the mystic is part.

Particularism and Universality in Abrahamic Mysticism

One might suppose that within the diverse mystical traditions there would be a good deal of specificity that would exclude those not part of a particular faith from aspiring toward the *sacer*. That exclusiveness would seem even more obvious for those seeking the innermost recesses of the *sacer*. To a certain extent that is true within the history of Abrahamic mysticism. Thus it would seem inherently impossible for a non-Jew to engage seriously in kabbalah, the central phase within the history of Jewish mysticism, since in order to be a practitioner one is expected to be an unequivocal devotee of the Torah, to understand every syllable of its text that is considered the unadulterated word of God and to believe that within and around every syllable there are God-intended *sacer* secrets waiting to be ferreted out.

Moreover, the methodology of ferreting out those secrets in kabbalah evolves, over time, with ever-increasing focus on the Hebrew letters—their numerological values, and eventually their sounds and even their shapes—that comprise the text of the Torah. So any aspirant to the *mysterion* whose doorway to that *sacer* interior is the Torah, would also need to be deeply versed in the linguistic and related aspects of the Hebrew language, a condition less than more likely for a non-Jew.

Similarly, Christian mysticism, for which the role most obviously equivalent to that of the Torah for Jewish mysticism is the figure of Jesus, would seem inherently to require of its practitioners that they believe completely and without hesitation in the divine nature—more accurately, the paradoxically fully human and fully divine nature—of Jesus. Regardless of other details, that essential starting point would exclude non-Christians for whom Jesus is maximally a prophet, and minimally not even a prophet, but certainly not divine.

One could argue as well, that Muslim mysticism must require of its practitioners that they embrace not only the *sacer* as Islam does (the sense of the *sacer* for Islam is virtually identical to what it is for Judaism; Christianity's understanding of Jesus as divine, and therefore of God as assuming human form at a particular moment in history for a particular—salvational—reason, offers a divergence from the other two Abrahamic systems of belief), but that they embrace the role of Muhammad as the final and consummate sacerdotal messenger between God and humanity, the ultimate *nabiyy* and *rasul*—which embrace will not be found among non-Muslims.[3]

Could a non-Christian, who does not read the Gospels with an urgent sense of their definitive quality, or a non-Muslim, who does not believe the Qur'an to be the ultimate word of God mediated through the ultimate prophet, expect to gain access to the *mysterion* by way of Christian or Muslim mystical thought?

Moreover, in the mystical traditions found in each of these three sibling faiths, there is an extraordinary range of diverse and different "schools" or methods of seeking the *mysterion* and/or modes of understanding what the essence of the *mysterion is*. Jewish mysticism goes through a series of phases that offer different emphases; Christian mysticism offers a large series of practitioners with divergent legacies of experience and instruction; Muslim mysticism—Sufism—offers a wide range of "orders"—*tariqas*—that have attracted diverse followings across time and space.

Yet one of the interesting aspects of the Abrahamic traditions is that, again and again one finds leading representatives of their mysti-

---

[3] The Arabic words *nabiyy* and *rasul* are typically if inadequately translated into English as "prophet" and "messenger" respectively. What mainly distinguishes them as terms is that, whereas both refer to individuals who serve as conduits through which God speaks to humankind, only a *rasul* ultimately leaves an important text filled with God's words as a legacy.

cal movements who, far from digging deeper into a particularistic view of the relationship between the *sacer* and ourselves and of how optimally to access that relationship, and committed as they are to their own particularized senses of what the *sacer* is and how to approach it most effectively; recognize that there are diverse paths to the same goal. Any number of these figures champions the notion that the *mysterion* may be accessed by individuals with varied perspectives regarding what it is and how to get to it, or that mystical aspirants from within the varied religious traditions can follow the path toward communion with the *mysterion* without abandoning their traditions to use methods outside those traditions.

There is an inherent logic to this: if my initial goal is to be filled with God in fusing with the *mysterion*, then I can only hope to do that if I empty myself of my *self*. In doing that, I empty myself of ego and therefore of the cocksure certainty that my way and only my way of finding the *mysterion* and my understanding of the *sacer* offer the correct way and the correct understanding. And if my *ultimate* goal in pursuing this initial goal is to return from my ecstatic experience as an instrument for working in partnership with God to perfect the world, then imagining that such a task can only be accomplished through means and methods that I prescribe would both be ego-embedded and reflect a failure to recognize the spectacular diversity of God's creation—the splendid diversity of ways in which humans find their way in the world and seek the paths beyond our world.

Thus, for instance: Abraham Abulafia, (1240-91)—born in Spain in the very year in which Rumi, in his pre-mystical years, was becoming recognized as an Orthodox scholar—asserted at age 31 that he had received the prophetic call, hearing a voice calling "Abraham! Abraham!" to which he responded: "Here am I!" (recalling that brief dialogue that sets *Genesis* XXII, and the offering up of his son to which the biblical Abraham is called, in motion). Shortly thereafter Abulafia began to gather a circle of pupils around him in his home town of Saragossa. He claimed to be able to train his pupils in what he called "Prophetic Kabbalah" (*Kabbalah N'vooeet*) through an intimate investigation of the Names of God to purify their souls and ultimately to achieve the capacity to exercise magical powers. The disciple's access to God's Names is through the letters comprising the names into which s/he absorbs him/herself, feeling inspiration (*in-spirit-ation*): s/he becomes possessed by God's name.

Abulafian *Kabbalah*'s underlying principle is that meditation on any letter within a word that addresses an aspect of the creation transmutes into a meditation on the whole of that word, and by further analogy, on the whole of creation and ultimately on the Creator. Such a deconstructive method of meditation—emphasizing most particularly the word of God: the Torah and, more broadly, biblical words and phrases—necessarily yields irrational meanings. Words and phrases are deprived of their everyday sensibility and thus function as a mechanism of guidance out of the here and now into the Other Realm in its deepest recesses: the more irrational, one might suppose, the deeper. The process is at once physical and mental. One begins with *mivta*: the articulation of the sounds of the letters. But not in a simple manner. Take, for example, the first letter of the Hebrew alphabet, *aleph*, which is part of the hidden divine name,[4] and repeat it in combination a) with each of the four letters of the *Tetragrammaton* (YHVH); and b) with every possible permutation of the five Hebrew vowels. The result is 200 non-sense sound-combinations.

As in other systems that emphasize dwelling on or repeating sound combinations—not only in Sufism or the hesychastic Christian mystics, but also in Hinduism and Buddhism—breathing is an essential element, and Abulafia offers instructions regarding how properly to breathe in the course of this process. Similarly, specific hand movements are to be performed during this process.

Much of Abulafia's terminology is derived from Greek, reminding us that he and other Jewish mystics of the thirteenth century, living cheek by jowl with Christians and Muslims in Spain in particular, were open to non-Jewish sources of potential wisdom where esoteric

---

[4] As he explains in his *Or haSeykhel* (*Light of the Intellect*) (MS Vatican 233, fol 97a). For much of the discussion of the next two paragraphs, see in particular Moshe Idel, *The Mystical Experience in Abraham Abulafia* (Albany: State University of New York Press, 1988) for more detail.

affairs were concerned. And most relevant to this discussion, Abulafia proclaimed his ability to teach outside the normal "canon" of kabbalistic discipleship. Typically, Jewish mystical study was limited not only to Jews but to *married Jewish males of a mature age with families*. But Abulafia claimed that he could teach his techniques to *anyone* with sufficient interest and will. He asserted that anyone—young or old; male or female; Jew, Christian or Muslim—could achieve the prophetic heights within the depths of the Divine *mysterion*.

Abulafia's consistent interest in and embrace of non-Jewish (and non-male) students was not conversionary: he believed that anyone with a strong enough ambition for accessing the *mysterion*, properly disciplined and properly instructed by him, could achieve that ambition. To believe that, he understood that access to the *mysterion* was not dependant on one's being Jewish, Christian or Muslim. His legacy would extend into the next phases of Jewish mysticism through the next six centuries. Moreover, through his universalistic thinking, Abulafia's influence would receive from and extend into Muslim mysticism and push toward the work of Renaissance-era Christian mystics such as Pico dela Mirandola.[5]

A generation before Abulafia's birth, St. Francis of Assisi (1181/2-1228) offers a different angle of grasping the reality of myriad paths to the singular, universal Divine *mysterion*. St. Francis offers a particularly interesting instance of such a perspective. On the one hand, he may be seen as the consummate exemplar of a Christo-centric mystical tradition. After all, he offers the most renowned instance of being so intensely wrapped within the *mysterion* that, emerging from it his very body was marked by the marks—*stigmata*—of Christ's physical wounds. These symbols of Jesus' self-sacrifice on behalf of humanity remained painfully imprinted on the saint's own body for the remaining few years of his life.

On the other hand, St. Francis is equally renowned for the intensity of his panhenotheism: the sense of God's presence in all of His

---

[5]   See Ori Z. Soltes, *Mysticism in Judaism, Christianity and Islam*, (Lanham, MD: Rowman & Littlefield Publishers, Inc, 2008), 222-4.

creation—the one (*heno*) God (*theos*) in everything (*pan*)—accessible, therefore, through communing with the trees and flowers, the birds and insects, the sun and the wind. His prayer to brother sun and his preaching to the birds are among the best-known of the writings ascribed to him.[6] For some panhenotheists it is easier to love the Creator through loving the animal and vegetal elements of the creation than through fellow humans, particularly if the latter disagree with one regarding how to understand and approach the *sacer*. Not so St. Francis: he became completely comfortable with all of God's creatures, human and otherwise. His love of humanity pushed him to travel and to encourage his acolytes to travel beyond their own small community not only across the countryside of central Italy, but across the world—including the non-Christian world.

In an era where the sword was the preferred instrument of Christian-Muslim contact for most men of the cloth and not only men of the world, he sought to bring his clear sense of the *sacer* to the *dar al-Islam* by the word alone—was even willing to risk losing his own life in order to speak with Muslim leaders and convince them of the spiritual Truth as he understood it. But his contemporary biographers speak less about his speaking about his *Christian* understanding of the *sacer* than of his listening to *Muslim* perspectives: remarkably, what he is famously said to have engaged in with the Emir of Egypt was a *dialogue*—a *colloquium caritatis*, a colloquy of mutual respect and even love—rather than a spiritual *debate*. So both principals in that discussion were engaged not in conversionary activity but in spiritual information-gathering with regard to diverse perspectives on God.

Abulafia and St. Francis offer two examples—and there are others—of Jewish and Christian mystics who exemplify the principle of thinking and feeling outside the box of one's particularized faith in seeking, or perceiving modes of seeking, the *mysterion*. And the same is true within the Sufi tradition. This is particularly distinct in the writings of Ibn al-'Arabi (1165-1240), an older contemporary of St. Francis, born,

---

[6] It is important to distinguish *panhenotheism*—the recognition of how the One God is manifest throughout creation (because God created it all)—from *pantheism*, in which some or all of the diverse forces of nature are understood to be divine.

like Abraham Abulafia, in Spain. Ibn al-'Arabi is arguably the first Sufi thinker to very specifically articulate a panhenotheistic understanding of reality. For, he points out, the Qur'an itself notes that "wherever one turns, there is the Face of God,"[7] and thus it asserts that "The Universe is God's form... [The aspects of] the Universe are manifest reality." God is what the universe makes manifest, so that the notion that the One Who "is also the inner essence [of those aspects] Who is Himself the unmanifest"[8] makes logical sense. Yet "He is Being itself; the Essence of Being," and thus impossibly beyond our grasp (for we cannot grasp pure Being).[9] Thus God is simultaneously immanent within the world around us and yet more transcendent than the most distant star.

The paradox is simple in its perfect impossibility. Since "He is the Observer in the observer and the Observed in the observed,"[10] and since ultimately "thou art not thou; thou are He" and "thou are not what *is* beside God,"[11] then it is a matter of finding one's self, finding [the manifestations of] God within one's self and finding one's self in his or her journey toward and with God—and the instruments of discovery are all around us in the myriad elements of the creation. Achieving the goal of being in intimate company with God is made possible by *recognizing* that one can *achieve* that goal, by recognizing the *availability* of instrumentation—which means rising beyond the everyday manner in which we look at the elements of the universe around us; emptying the mind of its *profanus* relationship to reality; seeking simultaneously within and without (and understanding that these "directionalities" are one and the same). Ultimately, "he who knows himself understands that his existence is not his own existence, but his existence is

---

[7] Qur'an II.115.

[8] Ibn al-'Arabi, *Bezels of Wisdom*, (Mahwah: NJ: Paulist Press, 1980) chap X, 92, 135.

[9] The quote is from *Bezels*, X. The issue of God as pure being is precisely parallel to that around which Jewish mysticism not only centers, but focuses with respect to God's name, YHVH, in Hebrew, the root of which word is "to be." For Sufism the issue does not focus on the linguistic content of the name of God, since the name/word "Allah" is not built from an Arabic language root that means "to be."

[10] *Bezels*, Ibid, 184.

[11] Ibn al-'Arabi, *The Treatise on Being*, W.H. Weir, transl. (London: Beshara Publications, 1975), 10.

the Existence of God."[12] That individual becomes the Complete, Perfect Man (*al-Insan al-Kamil*).[13]

Those who find God and verify their success at having found God (he calls these individuals *al-Muhaqqiqun*—"the Verifiers") remove the veils that prevent them from recognizing the God within themselves—from recognizing the fact of their *being* God. They are the People of Unveiling and Finding—*ahl al-kashf wa'l-wujud*—who have moved beyond the veils separating us from God. They have found what is always there, within themselves, falling first, in the discovery, into bewilderment (*hayra*). For this requires a different mode of thinking and feeling and sensing from those that we use in the *profanus* of the everyday. Indeed, it means to have arrived at finding and knowing God and at not-finding and not-knowing God at the same time. (For how can anyone *find* or *know*, with respect to God, in any ordinary sense in which we would use those verbs?)

But the *muhaqqiqun* are fully cognizant of the impossible paradox of their situation. It is not merely, then, that the One God is completely *other* than and yet *within* everything within the *profanus*, but, as we find/don't find and come to know/not know, then we can say: *huwa/la huwa*—"He is/He is not"—and in any way that we speak of "is" in the *profanus* and the language that is used in the *profanus* such a statement will be self-contradictory and therefore illogical.

There is more to this sense of paradox. Ibn al-ʿArabi asserts that all that exists—from Being itself to all of creation—exists due to God's will. God's agents for bringing that which exists into being are the Divine *Names*. One must imagine a process of *emanation* from the singular absolute God, through the multiplicity of Names that are and are not the same as God Itself, out into the realm of universal concepts and thence further "out": into the temporal universe being shaped in time

---

[12] Ibid.

[13] Given that Muhammad, Seal of the Prophets, is the one understood to be *al-Insan al-Kamil*, then we understand the implications of Ibn al-ʿArabi's comment: every mystic has the potential to become like a prophet—a *sacerdos* through whom God communicates to the *profanus*. This is of course consistent with what all the mystical traditions assert as their aspiration: to become sacerdotal conduits analogous to the prophets.

and space—but eternally extant in God's Mind. But of course the names—the words *we use and refer to* as Divine Names—are not the Names (as God would "know" them), but merely the "names of the Name" (*asma' al-Asma'*) that God has revealed through the Qur'an and the *hadith* to those who are intimately connected to God:

> ... The Divine Names that we have are the names of the Divine Names (*asma' al-Asma'*). God names Himself by them in respect to the fact that He is the One-who-reveals-by means-of-His-speaking (*al-Mutakallim*)... God says [in Qur'an 17:110], "call upon God [Allah] or call upon the All-Merciful; whichever you call upon, to Him belong the most beautiful of Names." Here God makes the most beautiful Names belong equally to both "Allah" and "All-Merciful." But notice this subtle point: Every Name has a meaning [*ma'na*] and a form [*sura*]. "Allah" is called by the Name's meaning, while "All-Merciful" is called by the Name's form. This is because the Breath [*Nafas*] is ascribed to the All-Merciful, and through the Breath the Divine words become manifest within the various levels of the void (*'adam*), which is where the universe becomes manifest. So we call upon God by means of the form of the Name.

There is thus a play on "Breath" (*Nafas*). God "says"—with whatever the Divine equivalent of "Breath" actually *is*—the entities that thereby come into existence. (God *says* the universe into existence: "let there be...").[14] It is the Breath of God that *besouls* beings, thus making them live and thus populating the universe with an endless array of them—the universe is both reified and animated[15] by God's Breath. And it is with our breath that we say the things/words that we say, including the Names of God. Thus, further,

> every name has two forms. One form is with us in our breaths and in the letters we combine. These are the Names by which we call upon Him. They are the "names of the Divine Names" and are like robes upon the Names. Through the forms of these names in our

---

[14] One not only recognizes the identity with Jewish and Christian thinking regarding Divine animation/besoulment of beings as part of the creation process recounted in *Genesis* I, but the precise cognate between the Arabic *nafas* and the Hebrew *nefesh* to refer to the breath that God breathes into the clod of earth (*adamah*, in Hebrew) to yield the first human being (*Adam*).

[15] From the Latin *"anima"* meaning "breath" and also meaning "soul."

breaths we express the Divine Names. Then the Divine Names have another kind of form within the Breath of the All-Merciful, with respect to the fact that God is the Speaker [*al-ka'il*] and is described by speech [*al-kalam*]... The forms of the divine Names through which God mentions Himself in His speech are their existence within the All-Merciful...

In Ibn al-'Arabi's notion of universal concepts (expressed and shaped by the Names) one may also recognize a relationship to Platonic thought and its discussion of the Forms.[16] Most important—and hardly surprising—for our discussion, within this part of Ibn al-'Arabi's far-reaching thought and writings is a clear statement of who it is that might achieve the goal of merging with God: anyone. For

> ...My heart can take on any form:
> A meadow for gazelles,
> A cloister for monks,
> For the idols, sacred ground,
> Ka'ba for the circling pilgrim,
> The tablets of the Torah,
> The pages of the Qur'an.

Aspirants of diverse spiritual traditions can become one with God. The heart to which he refers is both his heart, assumed an omnimorphic condition—and the heart of God. For if we understand this fragment from one of Ibn al-'Arabi's poems to refer to his condition once he has succeeded in achieving oneness with the *mysterion*, then his heart is emptied of himself and filled with God. So it is God who refers to Itself as omnimorphic with regard to those seeking God.

* * * * *

Thus as we shall see in more detail when we arrive at the discussion of Rumi's thought, a universalistic perspective with regard to the mystical process will already be well embedded in aspects of the Sufi tradition of which he is part, just as it may be found in parts of the Jewish and Christian mystical traditions.

---

[16] See below, chapter one, fn #37.

Chapter One

Sufism within the History of Islam:
From Rabi'a to Ibn al-'Arabi

The term commonly used to refer to Muslim mysticism is Sufism. The Arabic word *suf* means "wool" and the designation "*al-sufiya*," referring to someone who wears a simple woolen garment, may first have been used by Ibn Sirin of Basra (653-728/9)[17] to criticize those who prefer wool to cotton as the material for a simple garment.[18] But the wearers of simple brown woolen garments who are the beginning and backbone of the Muslim mystical tradition use the self-referential term to underscore both the simple

---

[17] The Muslim calendar begins with the *hijra*—the migration of Muhammad and his followers from Makka to Yathrib (Madina) in 622. Moreover, because the calendar is essentially lunar, the Muslim year of alternating months of 29 and 30 days, in which the last month of 29 days is extended to 30 days during leap years, is 354 to 355 days long, (in a 30-year period, there will be 19 regular years of 354 days and 11 leap years of 355 days) and it thus obviously completes itself approximately 10-11 days more quickly than does the Gregorian year. Thus the comparison of Gregorian and Hijra year numbers is not accomplished simply by adding or subtracting 622. To obtain the Hijra year from the Gregorian year, one must subtract 622 (actually, 621.57) and then divide the result by 0.97023. Approximate results would yield, for example, the year 1182 on the Gregorian calendar as the year 577 on the Muslim calendar; the year 1234 is the year 632, and so on. For simplicity's sake—because I assume that the vast majority of my readership is likely to be more familiar with the Gregorian calendar—I will use Gregorian dates throughout this narrative.

[18] Ibn Sirin accused them of trying to emulate Jesus in wearing wool, whereas, he asserted, the Prophet dressed in cotton. Thus it appears that in the late seventh or early eighth century there was a group of ascetics in Kufa (a city in Iraq where the Arabic calligraphic writing style, "kufic" developed) called *al-Sufiya*. Two hundred years later woolen garments had become the standard sartorial mode of Muslim ascetics throughout Mesopotamia, and the term "Sufi" was being applied to all Muslim mystics.

purity of their approach to the *sacer* and the completeness with which they have pushed aside material concerns. Perhaps the first individual actually to be called a Sufi and who also built the first Sufi *Zawiyyah* (a retreat house for mystics)—in Syria—was Abu Hashim from Kufa (d. 767 CE).

The term "Sufism" suggests the ascetic side of Muslim mysticism's beginning point, yet the mystic's goal grows from mere asceticism and an emphasis on fear or awe of God to the sense that such feelings are a starting point on the path that leads to fuller love of God—*mahabba*. The sources of inspiration and emulation are, in the first place, Muhammad himself, the ultimate Prophet intimate with God—and thus the source for grasping Muhammad is the Qur'an, God's word to and through the Prophet—but also the hadith (words of or concerning Muhammad) as well as the *awliya* (sing: *wali*). These last are the companions, both of Muhammad, and, over time, of God. They are similar to what saints are in the Christian tradition.[19]

Muslims are reminded by Muhammad, in the Qur'an, Sura 3:31, to "love God..." and it is that commandment that, from early in its formal shape, Sufism seeks to fulfill. The goal of the Muslim mystic may in fact be articulated within the parameters of a trio of terms—love, lover and loved one—and the notion that they describe a continuous circle, without seams and without beginning or end. Thus love binds the lover (the mystic) to the beloved (God) but when the goal of perfect spiritual love which is perfect spiritual union has been achieved, then the beloved becomes the lover and the lover becomes the beloved—or rather, they are both *both*, and the over-arching love (*mahabba*) that unifies them cannot be distinguished from either of them any more than they can be distinguished from each *other*.

The process of moving from separation to union is a spiritual pilgrimage through what, over time, various Sufi mystics will delineate as a series of stages (*maqamat*; sing. *maqam*) and states (*ahwal*; sing.

---

[19] It is a (Western) convention to render "*wali*" as "saint," just as it is a convention to render "*Rasul*" as "Prophet," but perhaps a more accurate rendering of the first term would be "friend," just as the second is better rendered as "Messenger of God."

hal) which, continuously marked by *dhikr*,[20] when also marked by *karamat* (graces) define that special relationship with God articulated as *baqa* (eternal continuance), *tawakkul* (sincere trust) *fana'* (passing away of one's self) and intense *rida* (satisfaction). This series of four aspects of where and how the mystic arrives at perfect spiritual union with God is itself circular: *baqa* leads to *tawakkul* which leads to *fana'* and to *rida*; but *rida* may be said to lead to *fana'*, *tawakkul* and *baqa*.

In the second and third centuries after the *hijra*,[21] as mystical doctrines began to shift more formally into place, the first shaping of monastic groups, dwelling in isolated cells and gathering for discussions of the Qur'an and hadith may be observed; and with reading aloud from these texts, the idea of the *dhikr* began to achieve prominence. So, too, the direction of Sufi thought began to shift from an emphasis on God's awesomeness to a passion to explore and express God's loving relationship with humans.

Rabi'a al-Adawiya (d. 801) is among the most significant of early Muslim mystics in general and in particular with regard to turning away from the fear and awe of God articulated by the previous few generations of Muslim ascetics toward the notion of achieving closeness to God through love. Rabi'a was a renowned mystic from Basra, who began to formalize the concept of *dhikr* in her own way as an ecstatic process *cum* center of seeking closeness with God's inner recesses, in which the gender of the mystic is irrelevant—as an alternative to the mainstream *masjid*, the male-dominated mosque as a house of prayer

---

[20] While this term is generally rendered to mean recitations from the Qur'an and hadith to shape a rhythmic liturgy, the term comes from the Arabic root meaning "remember." Thus its underlying principle is to use the slow and careful and repetitive recitation as an instrument to help the mystic keep God and the Prophet always before him. The emphasis on sound as a means to accomplish *dhikr*, since visual imagery might be more problematic, is suggested by the development of the *dhikr* into *sama'*: "spiritual concerts"—from the root of the Arabic word that means "hear." Eventually, as we shall repeat later, within the Mevlevi *tariqa*, the *dhikr* will evolve as more physical, a spinning that can sometimes continue for hours.

[21] This term refers to the migration of Muhammad and his initial group of followers from Makka to Yathrib—the town that would one day be called al-Madina—in 622, which event marks the beginning year of the Muslim calendar. See above, fn #17. As noted there, I am using the Gregorian calendar for all dates in this narrative.

and of study. "Love of God," she wrote, "has so completely absorbed me…" and further, she exclaimed that

> I love You with two loves,
> love of my [own] happiness [i.e., selfishly],
> and perfect love: to love You as is Your due.
> …that purest love, which is Your due
> is that the veils which hide You fall, and I gaze, adoringly, on You…

Rabi'a's articulation of the concept of selfless *mahabba* that would come to dominate Sufism over the next several centuries is—as the mystical process almost always is—fraught with paradox: one loves God because one ought to love God, not because it would give one satisfaction to do so, but how can it not be satisfying to do so? Isn't that what *rida* is? Yet—and this is part of the paradox—it is a *selfless* satisfaction. The issue is that, one loves God as one seeks oneness with God's *mysterion* not for one's own sake but for the sake of the community—the *profanus*—who will benefit from one's experience. Of course we are reminded, too, of the complications that apply to this front as well: getting there—to the depths of God—getting back from "there" and somehow expressing what is ineffable.

The intensity of connection to God, achieved by a *shaikh* through *fana'*, and defined as *ma'rifa*—a direct, personal experience of God rather than the "second-hand knowledge" (which is how *'ilm*—knowledge, was viewed by the mystics) provided by the traditional legalist leaders—opened a new set of spiritual possibilities, but also of threats to the mainstream leadership. It is not surprising, perhaps, that conflicts grew over the next two centuries—or that the mystic, Mansur al-Hallaj, a wool-carder, who exploded out of his experience of *ekstasis* by proclaiming how, emptied of himself and filled with God he could no longer identify himself as himself—so he blurted out *Ana al-Haqq*, meaning "I am Reality/the Truth" i.e., "I am God!"—was executed as a heretic in 922. That is: from the outside, his pronouncements were emphatically sacrilegious. From the perspective of a Sufi adherent, his assertions merely underscored the fact that he had successfully emptied himself of *self*, and become so filled with God that God was within the otherwise empty vessel of himself, rather than that he *qua* himself was God-*like*, much less God Itself.

It is largely due to the effort of two masters of Muslim jurisprudence who were eventually drawn to and became practitioners and champions of Sufism that the mystical tradition could be understood clearly not to contradict Islamic law. Thus through the work of Abu al-Qasm Abd al-Karim al-Qushairi (986–1072/4) and Abu Hamid Muhammad ibn Muhammad al-Ghazali (1058–1111) Sufism began to achieve a wider acceptance within the Muslim community and to spread, so that in particular from the late eleventh through thirteenth centuries new individual Sufi orders came into being, expanding further in the centuries that followed. First al-Qushairi and then al-Ghazali added significantly to the elaboration of the process of seeking and achieving oneness with the divine *mysterion*, by expanding and refining the detailed exploration and presentation of aspects of *maqamat* and *ahwal* that lead from *dhikr* to *fana'* and back.

Al-Qushairi's *Risala* began with a series of biographies of key Sufi thinkers and discussions of their thought. Thus his discussion of Hallaj, for example, reviews the latter's discussion of the Divine Attributes. He offers a series of statements associated with Hallaj, such as "All that appears through the body is necessarily an accident (*'arad*)" and "No 'above' shades Him—Exalted be He!—nor does any 'below' carry Him," and "No 'all' gathered Him," and "His description: He has none," and "If you ask 'When?'—His being is before Time… And if you say 'Where?'—His existence precedes Place… His existence is the affirmation of Him; Gnosis (*mar'ifa*) of Him is the upholding of His Oneness; and Oneness (*Tawhid*) is to distinguish Him clearly from His creatures. Whatever you imagine in your imaginings, He is different from that." Thus the very discussion of Divine attributes is intentionally futile; it is an exercise in the exercise of seeking to reach the unreachable and grasp the ungraspable.

From a discussion of earlier Sufis, the *Risala* moves to the discussion of technical terminology that has emerged in Sufi literature, such as the terms that distinguish *maqam* (stage) from *hal* (state). The distinction is fundamentally between the point (*maqam*) to which one arrives through one's own effort and that to which one arrives through the reaching "down" of God: each *maqam* "is an earning; each *hal* is a gift," the *Risala* states, as it then delineates 43 stages and states of mystical transcendence.[22] Thus one begins with *tawba*: "conversion" (in the Latinate sense of "intensely turning one's self"—away from a focus on worldly things and toward a life fully devoted to the service of God). The second stage is *mujahada*, meaning "struggle" or "striving" toward an intense spiritual—a mystical—life.[23] The third stage, "solitariness and withdrawal" (*khalwa wa 'uzla*) is an isolation and withdrawal from the community so that the beginner will succeed in his *mujahada* to achieve the fourth stage, *taqwa*, in which a full sense of awe of God furthers the mystic's resolve (since that sense of awe will help the mystic keep in mind the Divine chastisement that his newly chosen way of life will permit him to escape).

By the time the mystic has arrived at the sixteenth stage of his development as a transforming spiritual being he has arrived at contentment (*qana'a*) and in the seventeenth stage, complete *tawakkul* (trust in God): he has become like the prophetic figures, Abraham, Isaac and Ishma'el, who in the moment of Abraham's offering, exhibited absolute trust in God and therefore were able to offer a son or be offered by a father without a scintilla of question, much less protest, to God's commandment to do so.[24] By stage 21, the mystic is endowed

---

[22] Some readings of the *Risala* count up 45 of these.

[23] The term is derived from the same root found in the word, *jihad*, which in the vocabulary of everyday Islam refers to the struggle to perfect one's self as a *Muslim* (which term, we recall means "one who submits/surrenders" to God's will), to perfect the *Dar al-Islam*, and to perfect the world by causing it to recognize the Truth of Islam.

[24] We must keep in mind that, whereas in Judaism and Christianity it is a given that Isaac was the son who was offered, as described in *Genesis* 22, in Islam the Qur'an merely refers to "a gentle son" without specifying which one, and Muslim commentators debated which son it was for centuries. See Qur'an 37:100ff: "When he reached the age to work with him, he [Abraham] said, 'Oh my boy! Verily I have seen in a dream that I should sacrifice you; what then do you see [that is] right?' Said he [Isaac/Ishmael]: 'Oh my sire! Do what you are bidden; you will find me, if it please God, one of the patient!' So together they submitted [to God's will]..." And see, for example, the discussion by the eleventh-century scholar, Ath-Tha'labi, in his *Stories of the Prophets*, of the question of which son it was. He observes that

with *muraqaba*—constant awareness of God's Presence—and by stage 22 he is enveloped in *rida*: complete satisfaction. This "stage" is also regarded as the point of transition to "states", and is thus both the final *maqam* and the first *hal*—based on the Qur'anic verse: "God was well-pleased with them and they were well-pleased with God" (Qur'an 5:119). The sense of reciprocity expressed in this verse may be understood in at least two ways in al-Qushairi's interpretive context. The first is that humans arrive at satisfaction (*rida*) with God as and when God is satisfied with us. The second is that the understanding of *rida* as both *maqam* and *hal* offers a *structural* mirror of that sense of reciprocity: *maqam* becomes *hal* and *hal* becomes *maqam* when and as *rida* is felt from both the human and the Divine sides of the relationship—and "*rida*" is the particular term among the 43 delineated by al-Qushairi in which that reciprocity is most specifically articulated.[25]

What follows is a series of twenty-three states through which the mystic "progresses", beginning with *'ubudiya* ("servanthood"), a sense of complete subjection to the will of God. This *hal* should not be mistaken for an imperative to serve one's fellow humans, but rather to serve God. However, the idea of serving others will follow immediately, as *irada* ("desire")—the desire to abandon one's own desires and to fulfill only that which God desires—and a progression of five further states will lead to *hurriya* ("magnanimity"). Similarly, *jud* and *sakha'* ("generosity" and "givingness," together comprising #34 of the 43 principles) reflect thought and action toward others, inspired by the word of the Prophet in asserting that "the giving man is near to God, near to men, near to Paradise, far from Hell." Thus to be truly embedded within God is to turn one *toward*, not *away* from, one's fellows, but in a newly shaped, purer, realer, *truer* manner.

Ali and Umar had both asserted that it was Isaac, while others have asserted that it was Ishmael.

[25] There is also a more banal, historical-technical aspect of this discussion. Al-Qushairi explains that the Khorasanian School (in Iran) maintained that *rida* is a *maqam* that develops directly out of *tawakkul*, whereas the Iraqi school argued that *rida* is a *hal*. So his stance, he points out, is an intermediate one, in which the beginning of the experience of *rida* for the mystic is as a *maqam*, but the culmination of the experience is as a *hal*.

Du'a (informal prayer—as opposed to the formal prayer offered
five times daily in mainstream Islam, called *salat*), is reinforced by the
fact that the basis for the principle is the Qur'anic verse, "pray to Me
and I will answer you" (Qur'an 40:62). On the other hand, it is precisely the fact of emphasizing *du'a*, of suggesting a *constant* condition
of supplication before God and *constant* address of God that separates
Sufi doctrine as outlined by al-Qushairi from mainstream conduct.

The *Risala* proceeds through another four *ahwal* (states) before carrying the would-be mystic to the culminating *ahwal* (states) of *mar'ifa*,
mahabba and *shawq*. These last three interweave each other: the achievement of hidden knowledge comes into the heart, not the head, and
enters when the heart is perfectly still (as if the mystic were dead).[26] That
knowledge is indistinguishable from intense, perfect, real love in which
the lover, beloved and love itself are one and the same—in which the
mystic, God and the love of the one for the Other and the Other (who
is the *One*) for the one cannot be distinguished. The resultant condition, of having achieved God, is that one yearns never to be parted from
God. The dangers are apparent: that one dies, that one goes mad—for
one *cannot* return from the intimate recesses of the *sacer*—or, differently, where *mahabba* is concerned, that one apostasizes, turning away
from a proper relationship with God and the community.

For the layered notion of multiplicity with indistinguishable elements that are therefore part of unity might drive the mystic over the
precipice toward Christianity. If I embrace the notion that lover, love
and beloved are one, might I not embrace Father, Son and Holy Spirit as one? Muslim mysticism, having embraced the notion of a *mysterion*, accepts the paradox of unity that is yet somehow divisible between

---

[26] Some readers understand *tawhid* ([unequivocal belief in the] Oneness [of God]) to
be an underlying condition of Sufi understanding and *fana'* ("noble dying,") an
ultimate, underlying condition to which the Sufi arrives, so that these principles
should not be counted as part of the ladder of either *maqamat* or *ahwal*. Others
include these two, and understand them to be insertable as *ahwal* before the three
final *ahwal*—thus *tawhid* becomes #41 and *fana'* becomes #42—and/or, in another sense, as the final *transitional maqamat* that began with *rida*: as #23 and #24 of
45 "rungs" on the *Risala* ladder, rather than as two of an array of 45 Sufi *principles*
that encompass only 43 *Risala* "rungs."

its inner and outer aspects (or more aspects than merely these two). Thus from a mainstream perspective, mystics run the danger of even taking the further step, which would be to accept not only the idea of a tri-une God but the notion that one of the aspects of the indivisible, unaspected God is human in form.

The *Risala* is not only an obvious watershed in the history of Sufi theory because of its complexity and apparent contradictions. As a guide for the would-be Sufi it is a text that invites years of careful study, in part *because* of its contradictions, the embrace of which would be part of the shaping of a Sufi's spirituality.

Like al-Qushairi, al-Ghazali was, in his early career, a scholar of Muslim jurisprudence. Trained as an orthodox theologian and legal-ist, al-Ghazali was regarded as the most outstanding Sunni scholar of his era by the time he was appointed professor of divinity at the renowned Nizamiya Madrasa, in Baghdad, in 1091. Like al-Qushairi, he soon thereafter found the intellectual life that he led lacking in something essential—particularly in the application of a merely intel-lectual approach to religious matters. A mere four years after his appoint-ment, (in 1095), he resigned his teaching position and spent the next ten years in retirement and seclusion, seeking a more intimate relation-ship with God.

He lived a simple life, engaged in study and writing a series of books in which he explored aspects of the moral and metaphysical sys-tem of Sufism, which he sought to reconcile with orthodoxy. The cul-mination of his efforts to demonstrate that the fullest means whereby a Muslim may live a life of devotion to God is through Sufism, is the *Ihya' 'ulum al-Din* (*The Revival of Religious Knowledge*). In it, al-Ghaz-ali broadly solidified the position of Sufism within Islam, and more spe-cifically, re-introduced the notion of awe/fear that had dominated the beginnings of Muslim mysticism, albeit he did so from a different angle.

For al-Ghazali reminded the devotee of the horrors of hell, while validating the position of the *shaikh* as a guide the veneration of whom is based on his significance for the achievement of enlightenment by his pupils: "the disciple (*murid*) must of necessity have recourse to a mentor (*shaikh*) to guide him right. For the Path of the faith is obscure, but Iblis's [Satan's] ways are many and potent, and he who has no *shaikh* to guide him will be led by Iblis into *his* ways."

Al-Ghazali's *Ihya* divides the process of following the Path and achieving enlightened oneness with God into four aspects, each with its own elements. These four aspects are worship, personal behavior, the deadly sins, and the way to salvation. In an obvious sense, the first three areas of focus could easily apply to mainstream Islam without a mystical turn, except that parts of each suggest that turn. The fourth area of discussion in all ten of its elements connects to the specifically Sufi writings of al-Qushairi and other Sufi thinkers back to and beyond Rabi'a. Al-Ghazali highlights many of the *maqamat* and *ahwal* discussed in al-Qushairi's *Risala*, but adds elements of his own. The final two stages of the Path that he lays out are meditation (*tafakkur*) and the recollection of death (*dhikr*)—which brings the devotee full circle back to the notion of recollection (*dhikr*) as it applies to the awareness of God's eternal presence and the litany that reinforces that awareness.

We may all aspire to and arrive at the full awareness of God, that true knowledge of God hidden from those who do not pursue it assiduously:

> When the human being can elevate himself above the world of [relying on nothing but physical] sense, toward the age of seven, he receives the faculty of discrimination [*tamyiz*]…He then passes to another phase and receives reason ['*aql*], by which he discerns things necessary, possible and impossible; in a word, all the notions which he could not combine in the former stages of his existence. But beyond reason and at a higher level a new faculty of vision is bestowed upon him, by which he perceives invisible things, the secrets of the future and other concepts as inaccessible to reason as the concepts of reason are inaccessible to mere discrimination and what is perceived by discrimination to the senses.[27]

Moreover, God is eager to offer us a sense of where our trans-rational faculties can take us, if we allow them to do so, for "God, wishing to render intelligible to men the idea of inspiration, [i.e., being

---

[27] Al-Ghazali, *Munqidh min al-Dalal* (Deliverance from Error), [Translated as *The Confessions of al-Ghazali*,] (NY: Cosimo, Inc., 2010), 51.

inspirited with God], has given them a kind of glimpse of it in sleep."
But in order to carry the sort of experience which is glimpsed by the
sleeping unconscious mind, one must be free of doubts, which is not
that difficult, for

> [t]o believe in the Prophet is to admit that there is above intelligence
> a sphere in which are revealed to the inner vision truths beyond the
> grasp of intelligence, just as things seen are not apprehended by the
> sense of hearing, nor things understood by that of touch.

In the end, the intense proximity to God assures that the Sufi is a
true Muslim, [i.e., one who truly submits and surrenders to the will
of God], for "[t]rue knowledge…inspires in him who is initiated in it
more fear and more reverence, and raises a barrier of defense between
him and sin. He may slip and stumble, it is true, as is inevitable with
one encompassed by human infirmity, but these slips and stumbles
will not weaken his faith."

So, too, among the most significant Muslim thinkers of the era
that encompasses Rumi's thinking, both within the context of Sufism
and in broader Muslim thought, is the previously-mentioned Spaniard,
Muhammad ibn Ali al-'Arabi. Born in Murcia in 1165, Ibn al-'Arabi
also came to be known and commonly referred to as *Muhyi id-Din*—
"Reviver of the Religion"[28]—a symptom of how significant a figure
he was in the expansion of Muslim thought.[29] Ibn al-'Arabi was pro-
lific: he authored over 300 works, of which about 110 have survived in
manuscript form, perhaps 18 of these in Ibn al-'Arabi's own hand. In
these works he demonstrates a rich synthesis of intellectual acuity
with intuitive, visionary thinking, of legalistic and scientific learning
with experiential awareness. His mystical interpretations of Islamic

---

[28] More precisely, *"din"* refers to the legalistic aspects of Islam, as opposed to *"iman,"*
which term refers to the faith/belief aspects.

[29] Ibn al-'Arabi contributed broadly to Muslim thought, but he is primarily known for
his role as a teacher of Sufism; his name is often confused with that of a second
Ibn al-'Arabi, also from Andalusia, who was a scholar of al-Maliki jurisprudence.

doctrine are understood by his vast array of followers to have been divinely inspired to him as the "seal of the saints."[30]

After spending the first 35 years of his life in southern Spain and the *Maghrib* (Northwest Africa), Ibn al-'Arabi traveled as a pilgrim to Makka, where he ended up spending three years and was inspired by the aura of the region and his experiences within it to write his great work, the *Makka Illuminations* (*al-Futuhat al-Makkiyya*). Thereafter he moved about for a time in Syro-Palestine and Anatolia (Turkey), finally settling in Damascus for the remainder of his life. It was during this last, post-Makkan period that he married, raised a family, gathered an ever-growing circle of disciples, came to include key political rulers among those who sought his advice, and authored a steady stream of important works. These included *Bezels of Wisdom* (*Fusus al-Hikam*— which is often regarded as his greatest work; but others regard the 37-volume *Makkan Illuminations* as his greatest work); *The Contemplation of the [Holy] Mysteries* (*Mashahid al-Asrar*); and *The Book of Annihilation through Contemplation* (*Kitab al-Fana' fi'l-Mushahada*: this is a short treatise on the meaning of *fana'*: the annihilation of the self within the hiddenness of God).

One may recognize in Ibn al-'Arabi's thought the first clear articulation of panhenotheism within Sufism: the conviction that the one (*heno*) God (*theos*) can be found in everything (*pan*), since all of reality is the work of God and since if it is a given that a creator is embedded, one way or another, in that which s/he creates ("I see him in his painting;" "I hear her in her music"), then God must be embedded in Its creation. God is unequivocally One, yet the points of access to God are as infinite as the elements of our reality: one must merely understand how to use them as access portals. For, Ibn al-'Arabi points out, the Qur'an itself notes that "wherever one turns, there is the Face of God."[31] Thus to assert that "The Universe is God's form... [and that the aspects of] the Universe are manifest reality"— God is what the universe makes manifest, for God "is also the inner essence [of those

---

[30] This is a play, of course, on the phrase referring to Muhammad as the Seal of the Prophets.

[31] Qur'an II.115.

aspects] Who is Himself the unmanifest"[32]—makes logical sense. Yet "He is Being itself; the Essence of Being," and thus impossibly beyond our grasp (who cannot grasp pure Being).[33] Thus God is simultaneously immanent within the world around us, and yet more transcendent than the most distant star.

We cannot *see* God or in any sense *perceive* God or *know* God—because God is by definition beyond our senses, our sense of meaning, our knowing, our understanding: "None sees Him except Himself. None perceives Him except Himself. By Himself He sees Himself and by Himself He knows Himself."[34] He is inaccessibly hidden from us, but uniquely so: the veil that hides Him is not only part of Him, but indistinguishably, "His Veil is part of His Oneness."[35] The very terms, therefore—"veil" and "Oneness"—defy our understanding, who cannot conceive of a veil that is indistinguishable from that which it hides and cannot imagine a veil concealing something so completely that it is inalterably inaccessible to the senses or even the intellect. Yet it is the goal of the mystic—which goal is somehow achievable—to pierce, peer through, push aside that Veil that is not a veil behind which something is concealed, (for it is indistinguishable from the Oneness of which it is part), and cannot, by paradox, be pierced, peered through or pushed aside.

In Ibn al-'Arabi's notion of universal concepts (expressed and shaped by the Names of God) one may also discern a debt to Platonic thought and its discussion of the Forms.[36] This is further suggested by his discussion of the manner in which the elements of the *profanus* world, prior to coming into existence, were already present in God's Mind as *a'yan thabita*—"fixed prototypes." What obviously distinguishes these "prototypes" from Plato's Forms is that they intermedi-

---

[32] *Bezels*, X, 92.

[33] *Bezels*, X, 135.

[34] *The Treatise on Being*, 9.

[35] Ibid.

[36] I am referring to the notion that, for example, every just act participates in and emulates the Form "Justice" and every chair participates in and emulates the Form "Chairness."

ate between God and the Phenomenal world of which God is the Creator, rather than being the end/beginning point from which and to which all discussion of reality is ultimately directed (and which has nothing actively to do with the creation of the world).

Further, in Plato's understanding of reality there is a hierarchy of relationship to absolute reality: not only is the painting of a chair or a description of piety further from "chairness" or "piety" than a chair or a pious act is, (and thus not even worthy of study, due to their distance from the reality of their Forms), but "chairness" and "piety" themselves as Forms are lower than the ultimate Form, "the Good." We might assume that, in Ibn al-'Arabi's doctrines there would be a hierarchy of Divine Names, as there appears to be in the emanation-like process of creation referred to above. But since there is no hierarchy within the unified God, then "there can be no ranking in degrees in the Divine things, since a thing cannot be considered superior to itself...," and therefore

> There can be no ranking in degrees among the Divine Names, for two reasons: First, the relationship of the Names to the Essence is one relationship, so there is no ranking of degrees in this relationship... [otherwise] there would be superiority among the Names of God... Second, the Divine Names go back to His Essence, and the Essence is One. But ranking in degrees demands manyness. And a [unified] thing cannot be considered superior to itself.

Moreover, given the paradox of everything in the *profanus* already existing in God's Mind and God being manifest in all of reality, then the goal of the mystic is not to achieve *unity* with God, but rather to achieve full trans-cognitive *awareness* of *already* being one with the One. As with all of Muslim mysticism, the models for such a process are Prophets—except that Ibn al-'Arabi uses terminology that one may recognize as part of the continuum shared by all three Abrahamic disciplines with later Greek and Roman (specifically Stoic) thought: thus each Prophet is a *Logos* of God, a material manifestation of God's word, as each is a physical conduit through which God's word is articulated to humanity. The ultimate model—the *Logos* of *logoi*[37]—is the Prophet Muhammad; all other *logoi* (all individual previous Prophets) are united within the Reality of the Seal of the Prophets.

Those who find God and verify their success at having found God (he calls these individuals *al-muhaqqiqun*: "the Verifiers") remove the veils that prevent them from recognizing the God within themselves—from recognizing the fact of their *being* God. They are the People of Unveiling and Finding—*ahl al-kashf wa'l-wujud*—who have moved beyond the veils separating us from God. This requires a different mode of thinking and feeling and sensing from those that we use in the *profanus* of the everyday; indeed it means to have arrived at finding and knowing God and at not-finding and not-knowing God at the same time (for how can anyone *find* or *know*, with respect to God, in any sense in which we would use those verbs in ordinary parlance?). But the *muhaqqiqun* are fully cognizant of the impossible paradox of their situation. It is not merely, then, that the One God is completely *other* than and yet *within* everything within the *profanus*, but, as we find/don't find and come to know/not know, then we can say: *huwa/la huwa*: "He is/ He is not" in any way that we speak of "is" in the *profanus* and the language that is used in the *profanus*.

Nor is God's absoluteness a simple matter, in that God is both transcendent and immanent: "The Reality [*al-Haqq*—referring to God] of which transcendence is asserted [by us humans] is the same as the Creation (*khalq*) of which immanence is asserted, although logically the Creator is distinguished from the created"[38]—by definition: I and my painting, she and her poem are not one and the same; my painting resides in a gallery in Paris and I am here in Washington, her poem is being read by someone else in Moscow and she is asleep in New York City. But the point is precisely that one must *abandon* the *profanus* logic that applies legitimately enough to the *profanus*, if one is to grasp the inner recesses of the *sacer*. This does not render God any less than fully absolute; it renders God's absoluteness more complicated.

---

[37] Properly put, in Greek: *ho Logos ton Logon*.
[38] *Bezels*, 106.

That Reality is referred to as *al-Haqiqat al-Muhammadiya*—"the Reality (or Idea, or Truth) of Muhammad" or al-*Haqiqat al-Haqa'iq*: "The Reality of Realities." The Reality of Muhammad is spoken of as the Creative Principle and the Perfect Man is spoken of as the Cause of the universe—but they are one and the same, just as, by analogy, God and God's veil are one and the same, and just as God and God's Names are one and the same, and are not one and the same.[39] The Creative Principle sets the universe in motion; the Perfect Man is the epiphany of God's Will and Desire to be known. The Perfect Man— and he alone among humans—fully knows God and loves God and is loved in turn by God: for his sake the world was made and is maintained. The mystic who emulates Muhammad hopes to gain that knowledge and that love by achieving that perfection—which perfection will be the full recognition of being one with God, of loving and being loved by the awesome, transcendent God of infinite inaccessibility.

It might be noted that in his discussions, Ibn al-'Arabi, emulating Rabi'a, makes frequent use of the language of earthly love in his attempts to describe the condition of *ek-stasis/en-stasis* (not only because to leap out of one's self is to dive into one's self, but to embed one's self successfully into God's hiddenmost inner recess is merely to embed one's self deeply enough into one's selfless *self*, in the spaceless center of which God is found) toward complete merging with the Divine. The matter of recognizing what was true all along—that God is all around us and within us and that we are within God—which is true *fana'*, is to experience on an exponentially greater scale (and by means of a spiritual, rather than physical process, yet with a profound sense of physical consequence) the simultaneous death and (re-)birth which those perfectly in love experience.

In the generation of Ibn al-'Arabi and those generations following, three particular developments within Sufism might be noted. One is the growth of Sufi education centers toward providing systematic

---

[39] To say God's Name and thus make God present is and is not the same as if God were actually present, just as to say Bill Clinton's name and to discuss him is in some sense to bring him into the room, but not in the same way as if he were actually to walk into the room.

mystical instruction; these were modeled on the mainstream *madrasas*, but with a focus less on standard matters of Qur'anic jurisprudence than on the teachings of the Sufi masters. In an obvious retrospective sense one recognizes this dissemination of teaching through the proliferation of such centers (beginning in Persia and spreading mainly west toward Egypt and eventually across North Africa) as a fulfillment of the late twelfth, early thirteenth century dictum of Al-Ghazali that "the disciple (*murid/shagird*) must of necessity have recourse to a director to guide him."[40] Loose fraternities of mendicants—*fuqara* (in Arabic; singular: *faqir*) or *darvish* (in Persian)—began to emerge around a *shaikh/pir*. The residences of such masters thus began to function as entities akin to Christian monasteries, (in Arabic: *ribat*; in Persian: *khanqah*) growing through endowments from followers drawn to such centers for ascetic focus on prayer and concentration on the teachings of the master as the means of access to God's inner recesses.[41]

These centers continued to spread in the course of the twelfth and thirteenth centuries, providing guidance for initiates along the mystical path of *tariqa* (the "way"). Initiates into Sufi mysteries came to be marked by being invested with a special cloak—a *khirqa*—associated by tradition with a line of Divine service extending back to the Prophet himself.[42] Naturally, with such a widespread range of *ribat/ khanqah* structures, the variation of particulars with respect to *dhikr*, litany and doctrine also spread. Thus the second aspect of Sufi evolution during and beyond the time of Ibn al-'Arabi is the proliferation

---

[40] *Murid* is Arabic and *shagird* is Persian; the word that I am rendering as "director" is *shaikh* in Arabic and *pir* in Persian; it is more or less the equivalent of the well-known Sanskrit term, *guru*.

[41] The *ribat/khanqah* harbored ascetics, not celibates. Most Sufi masters were/are married—asserting that Muhammad himself (who was married, of course) proscribed celibacy (*rhabaniya*)—and in this feature they stand on common ground with Jewish mystics and on very different ground from Christian saints and mystics (for nearly all of whom celibacy is a given), although their organization as Orders invites obvious comparison with Christian monastic orders.

[42] We are reminded that the cloak is made of wool and that the term "Sufi" is arguably derived from the Arabic word for "wool"—*suf*—which material defined the garments of the early mystical ascetics of whom these communities are the spiritual descendants.

of the Sufi Orders—the word "Order" used here being the common-parlance, common usage meaning of *tariqa* (which is translated more literally as "way").

The eleventh-century Persian scholar, Hujwiri, already mentions several schools of Muslim mysticism associated with particular teachers, each with his own sense of the Way to access God's hiddenmost innermost recesses. Each *ribat* within each *tariqa* tended to include a double population within its ambience: the initiates and disciples who directed most of their time and energy to religious devotions and the practical matters of the *ribat* functions; and the lay-members connected to the *ribat* who participated in the *dhikr*) but lived outside lives with outside occupations and families.

Eventually, among this proliferation there emerges the *tariqa* associated with Jalaluddin Rumi. That *tariqa*, the Mevlevi *tariqa*, arguably became one of the renowned of *tariqa*s, both within and beyond the Muslim world. Indeed, part of what makes it such a focus of interest beyond the Islamic world is the universalist ideology that came largely to define it, an ideology shaped by Rumi, who is himself a student of earlier thinkers like Rabi'a, al-Qushairi, al-Ghazali and Ibn al-'Arabi. And Rumi himself will be a particular source of inspiration for Fethullah Gülen, as we shall explore in the chapters that follow.

Chapter Two

The Life and Thought of Jalaluddin Rumi

Mawlana ("Our Master") Jalaluddin ("The Glory of the Religion") Rumi lived in the middle of a most interesting and turbulent era, not only in the culmination of nearly five centuries of particularly profound developments within Sufi thought. The thirteenth century into which he was born was marked by major political upheavals in the Muslim world of the Middle East, most obviously the overturning of the Fatimid domination of Egypt and its environs by the Mamluk dynasty in 1250 and, more directly within Rumi's ambit, the final collapse of the Abbasid dynasty and the overrunning of its capital, Baghdad, by the Mongols, in 1258.

The Christian world was also undergoing a good deal of turmoil during the same century. It was a time of encyclopedic thinking: of varied attempts to encompass the entirety of human thought in vast compendia. Thus all of Christian thinking, for instance, is what St. Thomas Aquinas sought to include within his vast work known as the *Summa Theologica*; Jacob da Voragine focused on gathering and presenting the entirety of accounts of saints in his *Leggenda Aurea*; and Vincent de Beauvais attempted to address the entirety of human thought within the four components of his *Speculum Mundi*.

At the same time, substantial transitions in Christian art and architecture were in the process of leading from the Romanesque to the Gothic style. The Gothic cathedrals that resulted were visual encyclopedias, their vastnesses intended not only to suggest smaller versions of the universe itself—each a particularized microcosm of the macrocosm—but organized according to precisely proportioned arithmetic principles whereby every small detail offers a more miniature version of the larger parts of which each detail is ultimately part, so that the entirety functions as the kind of absolute order that is understood to define God's creation on the universal scale.

Part of what sets these new ways of thinking in motion—and others, ranging from the development of the musical scale associated with Guido d'Arezzo to banking systems—is that this same era marks the last phases of a formal series of Crusades, which had brought Christendom into violent, continuous conflict—but also cultural contact—with the Muslim world.[43] What began as a Christian attempt to wrest control of Jerusalem and other Middle Eastern sites from Muslim political control, by the thirteenth century was marked by a Crusade at the outset of the century (1201–1204) in which Western Christians went no further than Constantinople and the sacking of the capital of Eastern, Byzantine, Orthodox Christendom; to the questioning by the French King Louis IX (Saint Louis, as he is otherwise known), leader of the failed Seventh Crusade (1248–60) as to whether God is really interested in Crusades; to the "last" Crusade, which ended with the expulsion of the Crusaders from Acre, in 1291.

This is the complicated world into which Rumi was born on Sept 30, 1207.[44] His birthplace was Balkh, Afghanistan (part of the Khwarezmid Persian Empire) and he is therefore called Jalaluddin Balkhi by Persians and Afghanis. He is better known as "Rumi," which designation is derived from "Roman," for he and his father fled into what was called "Roman" Anatolia at the time of the first wave of Genghis Khan-led Mongol invasions (ca 1218–20) that virtually destroyed Balkh in 1219 and culminated with the fall of Baghdad in 1258. His moth-

---

[43] Thus, to offer one simple concrete example, the instrument that facilitated the functioning of a banking system, whereby one could place money into an account in one location and withdrew it in another (instead of travelling burdened with money), was the check; and not only the idea, but the very word came from the Muslim world. ("Check" comes through Arabic from the Persian term "Shah," meaning "king.")

[44] Some have argued that he was born in 1201 and still others that he was born in 1203. For the purposes of our discussion, his precise birth year is not important.

er is said to have been among those slain by the invaders;[45] he and his father came to Konya around 1220.[46]

Rumi's father, Baha ad-Din Walad, was a well-known theologian and jurist—he had been headmaster of a well-known *madrasa* in Balkh—whose reputation was sufficient for him to establish a successful school wherever he landed. From Balkh, the first significant stopping point for father and son was Nishapur, where the renowned Sufi poet—a member of the Kubrawiyyah or Zahabiyyah *tariqa*—Farid ad-Din 'Attar dwelled. The meeting between Baha ad-Din and 'Attar is legendary within the Sufi tradition both because of the sheer weight of two such esteemed and saintly figures, but also because 'Attar is said to have sensed the impending spiritual greatness of Baha ad-Din's son, the young Rumi. 'Attar presented him with a copy of his *Asrar-name*, and it is said that Rumi always kept that volume with him. Indeed, one of Rumi's better-known turns of phrase in his *Divan-i Kabir* asserts that "'Attar was the spirit, and Sana'i was his two eyes. We came into the realm of truth after 'Attar and Sana'i, following their footsteps."

From Nishapur, father and his son moved on to the Abbasid capital, Baghdad. There they were warmly received but stayed for no more than three days, for the grand city felt overly grand for their taste. From that point they followed the route of the holy *Hajj* (pilgrimage) to Madina and Makka, and then returned north, through Jerusalem to Damascus. They continued to Aleppo and thence to Erzincan, capital of the Mangujak dynasts. Again they were well-received—the Mangujak Sultan Fajr ad-Din Bahramshah and his wife wished to host them in the palace, but Baha ad-Din refused, wishing to stay in a *madrasa* complex as he always did.

Father and son continued to travel, on through Sivas, Kayseri and Nigde to Larende (now known as Karaman), where once again the local

---

[45] Others (notably, Ibrahim Gamard in his *Rumi and Islam*) have asserted that his mother died in Larende (present-day Karaman) not far from Rum, and therefore, presumably well after the family departure from Balkh.

[46] As the capital of the Seljuks of Rum ("Roman Anatolia") from 1071 through 1243, Konya was also called Rum.

ruler, Amir Musa Bey, invited the scholar to stay with him and was
politely refused—whereupon Amir Musa put into immediate action a
new project of building a new *madrasa* complex where Baha ad-Din
lived and began to preach. Here as in virtually all the places through
which they had passed along the way, the scholar taught, and the young
Rumi attended his father's lectures, heard his father's sermons and
also studied work by a range of other scholars, deepening his grasp of
the details of Islamic theology and jurisprudence.

Growing up in this ambience and following in his father's footsteps as he came of age, Rumi led the usual life for a religious scholar. A year after his father's death in early 1231, he found a spiritual
guide, in Sayyid Burhan ad-Din, a *shaikh* within the Kubrawiyyah Sufi
tariqa, who eventually advised him to go back to Aleppo and Damascus to study further. Rumi spent two years in Aleppo, in a Halwiyya
madrasa, studying Islamic jurisprudence with the most respected scholars in the area. In Damascus Rumi remained in a Maqdisiyyah *madrasa* for more than four years. This was during the period when Ibn al-
'Arabi, consummate master of Sufi thought, was also in Damascus—
the last four years of Ibn al-'Arabi's life there coincided with Rumi's
time there, and with what might be called the final stages of Rumi's
discipleship.

For by 1240, (the year of Ibn al-'Arabi's death and of Rumi's
return to Konya), Rumi had become recognized as a master of orthodox
scholarship. Four years later, stricken by a spiritual and emotional crisis—occasioned by the arrival of a Sufi, named Shams of Tabriz, whose
eccentricities and seemingly wild behavior attracted great attention, and
whom the young scholar embraced instead of shunning as others
did—he left orthodoxy behind in favor of mystical thought. He came
by that path honestly, since his father had a strong mystical side to go
along with his skill as a jurist; his (Rumi's father's) extant writings,
among other things, exhibit what for orthodox scholars was a shock-
ing sensuality in his description of his union with God.

Rumi studied his father's esoteric teachings, as well as the writings
of the Sufi poets Sana'i and 'Attar, through a former student of his
father's, Burhanaddin Mahaqqiq. Thus one might suppose that he was

predisposed to respond strongly when the wandering *darvish*, Shams, appeared in Konya/Rum and posed a question to the young scholar. Shams was a wild and wooly figure, reminiscent in his way of Diogenes of Sinope (412(?)–323 BCE), in ancient pagan Greece, who is said to have wandered around with a brightly lit lamp, during the daytime, asserting that he was "looking for an honest man." Shams had travelled throughout the Middle East, searching for answers to spiritual questions. It is said of him that at some point he heard a voice saying "What will you give in return [for answers]?" to which he responded: "my head," and heard further: "The one you seek is Jalaluddin of Konya."

In his *Ibtidaname*, the biography of Rumi written by his son, Sultan Valad, the meeting between Rumi and Shams is likened to the meeting of Moses and Khidr.[47] The *Ibtidaname* asserts that "when Rumi saw Shams' face, the secrets opened up for him. He saw unseen things. He heard things that he never heard from anyone. It was almost as if Rumi's shadow disappeared in Shams' holy light."

Shams appeared before Rumi and posed a question to him. Tradition, as it has primarily come through the *Ibtidaname*, has it that the question was "who is greater, the Prophet Muhammad or [the Turkish mystic] Beyazit Bistami, since Bistami asserted 'How great is my glory!'?"[48] whereas Muhammad acknowledged, in a prayer to God, that "we do not know You as we should." Rumi is said to have fainted. Recovering, he asserted that Prophet Muhammad was the greater, for while Bistami had swallowed one enormous gulp of God and stopped

---

[47] *Al-Khidr* ("The Green One"): some Muslims regard this figure as a righteous servant of God and others as a prophet. He is assumed by most to be the individual referenced in the Qur'an 18:65–82— (Sura *al-Kahf* ("The Cave")—whom Moses meets at the confluence of two seas and who asks to accompany Moses on board ship. During the voyage, al-Khidr's actions are so disturbing to Moses that he transgresses his vow not to ask questions on three different occasions. Al-Khidr is also referenced in the hadith and is a beloved figure in the Sufi tradition. See Michelangelo Chasseur, "Oriental Elements in Surat al-Kahf," in *Annali di Scienze Religiose* 1 (Brepols Publishers, 2008), 255–89.

[48] Bistami was speaking in the manner that we associate with Hallaj, meaning that "my" refers not to himself, but to God, since in his ecstatic condition he is completely empty of self and filled with God.

there, for Muhammad the *tariqa* ("path")[49] was always and continuously unfolding with new nuances and aspects.

But the dialogue that ensued between Rumi and Shams made of the two inseparable companions in the search for greater intimacy with God. Sultan Valad wrote "Shams of Tabriz and my father—may God bless the secrets of both—were among the elite of the most beloved servants of God. They were one person, one holy night, separate in appearance but one in truth." It was clear, though, that this intense friendship was making Rumi's position as an attentive teacher difficult, that Rumi was less inclined to bury himself in books and less accessible to those seeking his attention. Realizing that he was conjuring hostility from those around him for his "intrusion" in Rumi's life, Shams disappeared nearly 16 months after he had appeared. He went back to Damascus.

There followed a dark period for Rumi, culminating with some correspondence with Shams and then the dispatch of Sultan Valad to beg Shams to return to Konya. Shams returned, but soon once again the level of jealousy-bred hostility toward him escalated. That ugliness of sentiment, together with the sudden death of Shams' wife Kimia, not long after his marriage to her, pushed Shams away from Konya again: he disappeared in December, 1247 but this time nobody knows where he went—or if he was murdered (perhaps with the cooperation of another of Rumi's sons).[50]

Rumi was despondent: "he whirled day and night, and his crying was heard by all."[51] Even with Shams' abrupt disappearance, however, there was no turning back to his old style for Rumi. Indeed it may well have been Shams' disappearance that forced Rumi around the final turn toward his transformation as a mystic and as a poet who verbalizes

---

[49] Derived from the word "*tariq*," which means way or path, the word "*tariqa*", of course, comes to be used to refer to Sufi orders. Each "order" offers a particular *path* to the *mysterion*.

[50] There are two slightly different versions of his fate, one told in the *Ibtidaname* and one in Aflaki's fourteenth-century work, the *Manaqib al-Arifin*. See Shefik Can, *Fundamentals of Rumi's Thought*, 59-61.

[51] Ibid, 61.

his mystical quest in poetic terms. In his distress and in his new emotional excitement, he often underscored his teaching with whirling and skipping dance-like movements—appalling the many students he now lost, while attracting others.

Soon he became a *shaikh/pir* in his own right—so the well-respected scholar of 1240 became a renowned Sufi master by 1248, and the unique form of physical *dhikr* that must have begun during the 16 months of Shams' first presence in Konya and reached full efflorescence by the time Shams' last disappearance became "standardized" by that time. Rumi attracted followers into what evolved as his own *ribat* and his own *tariqa*. Due to the Turkish version of his Sufi name, that *tariqa* is perhaps best-known as *Mevleviya Tariqa*: the Mevlevi Order.

Shams as an alter ego appears in some of Rumi's poetry not only as himself, but as a symbol of the God and the Divine *mysterion* sought by Rumi and Shams through their intense, ongoing spiritual dialogue together:

> The soul's mirror is naught but the face of the friend, the face of that friend who is of that spiritual land beyond. When your eye became an eye for my heart, my blind heart went and became drowned in vision. I saw that you are the universal mirror unto the Everlasting; I saw my own image in your eye. I said, "At last I have found myself: in his eyes I have found the shining Way." (But) my image gave voice from your eye (and said), "I am you and you are I in (perfect) oneness."[52]

The "you" is both Shams and God: in finding the one Rumi finds the other and in both cases—which are, in effect, the same case—he finds himself. This is the *mahabba* of absolute *tawhid*.

The mirror of *mahabba* and *tawhid* would reflect two other key figures for Rumi's spirit and the poetry that flowed from it. Salah ad-din Zarqubi, the goldsmith, became the most important conduit for the poet's spiritual continuity some time after Sham's final disappearance. The *Ibtidaname* explains that "when [Rumi] found the holy light and reflection of shams [the sun] in Salah ad-Din, he said to his friends,

---

[52] *Divan-i Kabir*, (also known as *Divani Shamsi Tabriz*) Vol. V, #2492

'...from now on your *shaikh* is Salah ad-Din...' He called me [Sultan Valad] and said to me, 'Behold Salah ad-Din's face; he is Shams himself. Now you follow him, too.' ...I accepted my father's order eagerly..."[53]

Interestingly, Salah ad-Din was unschooled: the sort of spiritual wisdom he possessed and conveyed transcended literary and scholarly forms. Rumi addressed him, in one of his letters, as "*shaikh* of *shaikhs*, sultan of *shaikhs*, saint of God on earth, God's light among human beings..."—and in fact arranged a marriage between Sultan Valad and Salah ad-Din's daughter, Fatima Khatun.

Salah ad-Din became ill and died at the end of December, 1258. If once again Rumi was alone in terms of human mirrors of his passion for God, on the other hand "his ultimate purpose was not mortal friends. His aim was to be with true friends who loved God, in order to attain the True Friend, Friend of Friends."[54] But such friends seemed to serve to inspire him toward articulating that Friend of Friends and the path to the *mysterion* within Him. Some time after the death of Salah ad-Din, the pleasant task of filling that role fell to Husam Chelebi, Rumi's scribe and favorite student—in one sense the mirror opposite of Salah ad-Din: the one inspired poetry in Rumi that he himself could not read, the other was the one who wrote down much of the sea of poetry flowing from Rumi. Husam's importance to the ongoing development of Rumi's thought can be discerned simply by the fact that it was he to whom Rumi dictated the six volumes of the Mesnevi.

Within Rumi's passionate writing about being in the world, and about being—or longing to be—beyond our world in the innermost depths of God, this succession of close friends and inspirations appears self-reflexively. Thus, for instance, the passage

> ...Husam,
> Tell about the visions of Daquqi,
> Who said,
> "I have travelled East and West not knowing Which way I was
> going, following the moon, Lost inside God."

---

[53] Quoted in Shefik Can, *Fundamentals*, 69.
[54] Ibid, 76.

both informs us about the nature of the poet's "indirect" writing process, through Husam, and tells us about the process of his seeking to be lost within God: by seeking God everywhere and not within a confined realm. The direct implications of this poetic fragment are geographic (and after all, Rumi was somewhat of an itinerant, from the death of his mother to the time of his own death). However, the indirect implications which are elsewhere explicit, as we shall see, are that following the moon that shines on every corner of the planet is a metaphor for his embrace of any and every tradition and type of tradition in which seekers seek God.

The *Mevleviya Tariqa*, as we have noted earlier, became marked by a unique *dhikr*—a *dhikr* at once spiritual and physical—in which devotees not only whirl with increasing speed in concentric circles, but learn to whirl around individually for extended periods of time, with absolute, perfect equilibrium, so that they are able both to start and to stop abruptly and without a scintilla of balance unease. With one hand pointing down and one up, each whirling *dervish* is a microcosm of perfectly centered reality, of close-eyed inner sight, a perfect connector between earth and heaven, a simultaneously still and silent yet ever-moving, rustling access-seeker and -achiever to the hidden God.

Rumi undertook his own final *hijra*—his final migration—to the world of eternity, which is a phrase far more apt than one that speaks of his death, on December 17, 1273. His literary legacy includes, besides the *Mesnevi*, the *Divan-i Kabir*, *Fihi Ma Fih*, *Majalis-i Sab'a* and the *Maktubat*; other works are ascribed to him by some, but these are the works universally accepted as his works.[55]

The first of these consists of six volumes—25,618 couplets—that follow a singular form: every verse uses the same meter and each couplet offers its own internal rhyme scheme. It is filled with anecdotes with a moral lesson and often this follows a circular style such that

---

[55] There are variant spellings and titles for the first two of these works which are Rumi's most substantial, by far. Thus "*Mesnevi*" will also be found as "*Mathnawi*," usually depending upon whether the source is Persian or Turkish; and the *Divan-i Kabir* is also called the *Divan-i Shamsi Tabriz*, thusly named for Rumi's great friend and mystical inspiration, Shams of Tabriz.

one story leads into another (and sometimes a third) before returning to the original story and seeking its conclusion. The sources of these stories are culturally and spiritually diverse, adopted, adapted and shaped to the poet's purpose. The *Divan-i Kabir* ("Great [Poetry] Collection") is a compendium of poetry, mostly in Persian, but some also in Arabic or Turkish, in different formats. Whereas it was often a stylistic affectation of eastern Islamic poetry for the poet to incorporate his own name within a poem's verse, Rumi instead incorporates Shams' name, or occasionally the names (or nick-names) of Salah ad-Din Zarqubi or Husam Chelebi.

The *Fihi ma Fih* are versions of sermons—and parts of a commentary on the *Mesnevi*—given over the years by Rumi and written down by his son Sultan Valad or some other disciple. The *Majalis-i Sab'a* is a group of seven specific sermons given in different times and places after the death of Shams. Finally, the *Maktubat* is a compendium of 147 letters dictated by Rumi at various times to various state officials.

The Mevlevi Order flourished and spread in the course of the period from the fifteenth through the early twentieth centuries, in which the Ottoman Empire encompassed Turkey and other lands. As such, it often exerted strong political power by means of the influence of its *shaikh*s on Sultans and the wide circle of their governing infrastructure. Meanwhile, many other Sufi Orders—scores of them—developed across the Muslim world in the course of the thirteenth through early twentieth centuries.

* * * * *

If in some respects Rumi has come to be viewed as the Newton of Sufism, then like Newton, he "stood on the shoulders of giants" in order to gain his far-reaching view of humanity and its relationship to God. Among his predecessors none is more important with respect to a universalist viewpoint than Ibn al-'Arabi, whose panhenotheistic perspective was briefly discussed in the previous chapter.

Thus among the poems within the vast range of writings ascribed to Ibn al-'Arabi, one (already quoted, in part, in the previous chapter) in particular stands out as a concise reminder of his understanding of

God's even-handed interest and focus not merely on all of humanity, but on all of creation. He writes (in his *Fusus al-Hikam—Bezels of Wisdom*):

> Wonder,
> A garden among the flames!
>
> My heart can take on any form:
> A meadow for gazelles,
> A cloister for monks,
> For the idols, sacred ground,
> Ka'ba for the circling pilgrim,
> The tablets of the Torah,
> The pages of the Qur'an.
>
> My creed is love;
> Wherever its caravan turns along the way,
> That is my belief,
> My faith.

There are several issues of note for our discussion in these passages. We might begin by asking what the meaning could be of the second line of the poem. The flames might be understood to be our own world, an ever-burning reality that lacks solid spiritual substance and is constantly engaged in the act of consuming itself. But in the midst of that reality, the garden that alludes to the ideal paradise before and beyond our world toward which the mystic aspires—the aboriginal Garden in which Adam and Eve dwelled concerning which all of the Abrahamic traditions speak in terms of an ultimate return as a desideratum.

But it is the content of the next stanza that elucidates how to locate the doorway back to the Garden. It is a doorway of panhenotheism—one that sees God in everything. It is a path that recognizes that soaring out of oneself toward the *mysterion* in ecstasy may—or must—be synonymous with sinking deeply into oneself in enstasy, for the heart of God that the mystic seeks, in pure defiance of the directional logic of the everyday world, can be found both beyond the most distant elements of our universe and within each and every one of us, who are be-souled beings by virtue of God's breath within us from the outset of the creation of the universe.

The seeking of God's hiddenmost innermost recess within one's self, like the seeking of that *mysterion* outside one's self must be devoid of self if one is to succeed; to be fully filled with the love of God one must dissipate into God, be "replaced" in one's innermost being with God—become God. This is *fana'*—and this is what another, much earlier Sufi to whom Rumi often refers, Hallaj, said when he exclaimed, "*Ana al-Haqq*,"—"I am Being, God, It!" (The danger is that, like Hallaj, we cannot return to the self of ourselves; the danger is that others mistake the complete mergence with God as something else: a heretical substitution of the self for God.

The doorway into the Garden of the *mysterion*, moreover, is arrived at by many different paths. The multitude of these paths as Ibn al-'Arabi unfolds them lead through all of God's creation in its endless diversity. God will be found in everything created by God, whether a field that serves non-human animals as food and shelter and comfort or any number of contexts in which humans engage in seeking God. And as for humans, that Garden may be accessed from any number of starting points: not only Abrahamic traditions (Christian monks, the Jewish Torah, the Muslim Qur'an and Ka'ba), but also—*even*— those who worship idols.

How is this possible? How can the garden of God's *mysterion* be accessed from so many different directions? Because God's creed is love: God loves all of those created by God, and the *mysterion* is available to any who, in love—in true, absolute, unequivocal, perfect love— seek it. The voice of the poet ("my belief; my faith") is indistinguishable from the voice of God, for once he has merged with the Creator in love—once he has melted into God (*fana'*) then he is *al-Haqq*. Thus wherever the caravan of love originates and however it travels, by whatever route, that origin and that route are his belief, his faith—that route and origin lead to the *mysterion*, to the Garden in the midst of the flames that consume the world.

Ibn al-'Arabi, whose work was monumental enough for it to be virtually unignorable by any Sufi who came after him, may be seen, then, to provide an important foundation for the universalism so evident in the thinking and the poetry of Rumi. There is a wide range of ways in which Rumi's thinking is important both to the Sufi tradition and to the Muslim tradition on the one hand; and to the broader realms of human thought on the other. (And this, in turn, will be of significance, in particular ways, as we shall see, in turning to a discussion of Gülen's thought in relation to Rumi, to the broader Sufi and Muslim traditions, and to the relationship between all of these and the world at large).

Rumi is arguably the preeminent exponent of the idea promoted by Ibn al-'Arabi regarding God's universal, as opposed to Islamocentric (or any other sort of –centric) focus. One way in which Rumi expresses such universalism is by inclusive references to the Prophets—the Messengers, the *Rasuls*—reverenced in other traditions, who are presented in his poetry no less reverentially than is the Prophet Muhammad. Thus

> ... Spring is Christ,
> raising martyred plants from their shrouds....
>
> ...This wind is the Holy Spirit.
> The trees are Mary.
> Watch how husband and wife play subtle games with their hands....
>
> ...The scent of Joseph's shirt comes to Jacob.
> A red carnelian of Yemeni laughter is heard
> by Muhammad in Mecca. (*Divani Shamsi Tabriz* #2003)

Christ, the Holy Spirit, the Virgin Mary and the Israelite patriarchs Jacob and Joseph share the same territory with the founder of Islam. Jacob again appears—delineated once again by the grief for his lost son, Joseph (who is destined for greatness in Egypt, which locale will yield up the greatness of Moses, whose spiritual descendant is Jesus):

> Who gets up early to discover the moment light begins?
> ... Who, like Jacob blind with grief and age,
> smells the shirt of his lost son
> and can see again?
> Who lets a bucket down and brings up
> A flowing Prophet? Or like Moses goes for fire
> And finds what burns inside the sunrise?

Jesus slips into a house to escape enemies,
and opens a door to the other world.
Solomon cuts open a fish, and there's a gold ring.
Umar storms in to kill the Prophet
And leaves with blessings...

(Divani Shamsi Tabriz #598)

The same sort of prophetic-sacerdotal connection among these Prophets is shared between ruler-sacerdotal figures: the Israelite King Solomon and the Caliph Umar, one of the Prophet's companions—who indeed began as an enemy and ended as a friend, father-in-law and successor as shepherd of the Muslim flock.[56] The inner spirit can be interwoven with the outer world of politics, when those governing that outer world are rightly guided by the One with whom the inner-spirited ones seek oneness. There is more along these lines, for

... Moses, the inner light of revelation,
lit up the top of Sinai, but the mountain
could not hold that light....

...Joseph's brothers did not see Joseph's beauty,
but Jacob never lost sight of it. Moses at first
saw only a wooden staff, but to his other seeing
it was a viper and a cause of panic.[57]

Eyesight is in conflict with inner knowing
Moses' hand is a hand and a source of light.

These matters are as real as the infinite is real,
but they seem religious fantasies to some,
to those who believe only in the reality
of the sexual organs and the digestive tract...

(Mesnevi V, 3925 ff)

---

[56] 'Umar was the second of the four *rashidun*—"rightly-guided"—caliphs who immediately succeeded the Prophet: Abu Bakr, 'Umar, 'Uthman and 'Ali.

[57] For the purposes of our discussion I am ignoring (except for this footnote!) an obvious layer among the possible layers of meaning for Rumi's imagery of Joseph, Jacob and Joseph's brothers: that Joseph is a metaphor for Shams, Jacob a metaphor for Rumi and the brothers a metaphor for those who so vehemently—and in the end, perhaps violently—opposed Shams, failing to see the spiritual beauty that so captivated Rumi, who "never lost sight of it."

In the realm of seeking, inner sight counts for more than outer sight, and a range of prophetic beings from a range of traditions possess it. The potential to be lit up by the inner light of revelation is there for any and every seeker who seeks with the right kind of eyes. That potential is what distinguishes us—humans—from other species and other aspects of nature. For we are God's representatives or vicegerents on earth, as the Qur'an explains in 2:30—and to us is granted (upon us is imposed) this responsibility because mountains and other aspects of nature found such responsibility too heavy: the mountain could not hold that light.

Neither the love of God by the mystic nor the love of the mystic by God is confinable to one mode of conceiving God and God's message and one method of accessing God in God's hiddenmost recesses. For

> [t]he creed of love transcends the specific creeds of the different religions. We do not need to define true religion by statements of belief. We need only say that we are lovers of God. (*Mesnevi* II, 1770)

Rumi broadens his articulation of this principle by way of a parable regarding Moses, in the heart of which,

> … A sudden revelation
> came then to Moses. God's voice:
>
> *…Ways of worshipping are not to be ranked as better*
> *or worse than one another.*
> *Hindus do Hindu things.*
>
> *The Dravidian Muslims in India do what they do.*
> *It's all praise, and it's all right.*
>
> *…That broken-open lowliness is the reality,*
> *not the language! Forget phraseology/ I want burning*, burning…
>
> The love-religion has no code or doctrine.
> Only God.
>
> So the ruby has nothing engraved on it!
> It doesn't need markings… (*Mesnevi* II, 1750 ff)

Rumi reiterates this theme a number of times. He asserts:

... I go into the Muslim mosque
and the Jewish synagogue
and the Christian church
and I see one altar.

Surely the broadest expression of Rumi's universalism is contained in one of his best-known turns:

Not Christian or Jew or Muslim, not Hindu,
Buddhist, Sufi, or Zen. Not any religion

or cultural system. I am not from the East
or the West, not out of the ocean or up

from the ground, not natural or ethereal, not
composed of elements at all. I do not exist,

am not an entity in this world or the next,
did not descend from Adam and Eve or any

origin story. My place is placeless, a trace
of the traceless. Neither body or soul.

I belong to the beloved, have seen the two
worlds as one and that one call to and know,

first, last, outer, inner, only that
breath breathing human being.[58]

This is one of the ultimate statements of God as a universalist and of the idea that there are many paths to God in seeking oneness with the One. Moreover, the manner in which Rumi expresses himself—"my place...," "I belong," and so on—suggests that he speaks *as God*. We may recognize this readily enough as a Hallaj-like mode of self-expression: the speaker is both the mystic and God, the lover and the beloved, the seeker and the sought, because—and this is his main point—when the process of seeking oneness with the One has succeeded, both the distinctions among different types of seekers (Christians,

---

[58] Both this poem and the preceding fragment have long been ascribed to Rumi—and this is validated, among other reasons, by the large number of unequivocally attributed passages that convey the same sort of sentiments—although they are not found in the *Mesnevi* or in the *Divani Tabrizi Shams*.

Jews, Muslims, Hindus, Buddhists) evaporate and the distinction between the mystical self (emptied of self in order to be filled with God) and God dissipates.[59]

For, as the poet says elsewhere:

> ...Every holy person seems to have a different doctrine and practice, but there's really only one work. (*Divani Shamsi Tabriz* #258)

There is a still broader starting point and a similarly central aspect of Rumi's poetry that goes beyond human relations and how they are embedded in the matter of God and Divine-human relations. This is the multiple ways in which Rumi articulates the notion not only of universalism but of panhenotheism. Thus for example, he writes:

> Think of all creatures as pure and clear water, reflecting the attributes of God. Every creature possesses something of the knowledge, justice and kindness of God; they are like stars in the night sky reflected in flowing water.... Generations come and go, and each generation is a new generation, reflecting the Divine Attributes in a new way. Yet the attributes themselves do not change; justice is the same justice, and knowledge the same knowledge... (*Mesnevi* VI, 3172-6)

The notion of the Divine presence throughout creation could not be more eloquently expressed. Rumi verbalizes the eternality of that presence—its transcendence not to a place beyond human experience but from one generation to the next within the world that encompasses human experience.

Elsewhere, on the other hand—and not surprisingly—he addresses, among other subjects, the issue of God's *existence*, offering richly-articulated perceptions that would convince the unbeliever. For instance:

> How could the waves move and make foam without wind? How could dust rise from the dry earth without wind? Yet we cannot see the wind; we only infer it from its external forms. From every

---

[59] Put otherwise, were Rumi a non-mystic we would need to understand such turns of phrase as misguided, egotistical—and heretical in the extreme. But as a mystic, he speaks with the paradoxically Divine voice only as a symptom of having been drained entirely of self, of ego, and—momentarily—filled with God.

external form we can infer the divine spirit, the wind of God. (*Mesnevi* VI, 1459-60)

More broadly, he argues that the physical, tangible elements perceived by the senses not only offer only a part of the story of reality but don't offer even the most substantial part of it. Thus

> The unbeliever argues: "I can perceive nothing apart from what my five senses perceive." But the unbeliever never reflects that the perceptions of the senses give news of that which is beyond their perception; they pick up hints of hidden wisdom. Indeed the purpose of the five senses is to induce the individual to seek this hidden wisdom. (*Mesnevi* IV, 2878-80)

> God has made the outer worlds appear real; and he has made the inner worlds seem unreal. But these are disguises, since the opposite is true. In the same way he has hidden the sea, but made the foam visible; and he has hidden the wind, but made the dust visible. (*Mesnevi* V, 1026-7)

The conclusion of this sensibility is to

> [i]gnore the outward forms of things. Do not concern yourself with the names people give to things. The form of a thing is a gate; the name of a thing is a title inscribed on the gate. Pass through the gate into the meaning within. (*Mesnevi* I, 1285)

Moreover, as a mystic, he recognizes that the structures put into place by and for mainstream religion are insufficient for those—mystics—who would seek the innermost hidden core of God. Adherence only to the external forms of religion in its garden-variety, everyday state, yields only the outer edges, not the inner recesses of the *mysterion*—it is accessed by the mind and not truly by the soul.

> Intellectual knowledge about religious matters is the bane of the spirit. Such knowledge is like borrowed money; it does not belong to the person who possesses it. Yet those who amass intellectual knowledge about religion believe that they are acquiring religion itself. You must become ignorant about religion... (*Mesnevi* II, 2326-7)

This doesn't mean that religion, per se, is wrong—on the contrary, at its best it serves the purpose of improving Divine-human relations and thus the world:

> Malice is a plant whose roots lie in hell. The enemy of malice is religion. (*Mesnevi* II, 274)

It's just that in its overly priest-dependant form it falls short of what the mystic wants to achieve. The mystic's goal is to so entirely mind-meld with the *mysterion* that such guidance and intervention that sacerdotal intermediaries offer are not necessary—are in fact obstacles to complete merging. For

> [t]o encounter God is like meeting your lover; you have no more need for go-betweens carrying messages. (*Mesnevi* IV, 2068-9)

And what is the goal within that goal of oneness with God? It is release from the fetters imposed upon us by excessive attachment to the here and now and its material concomitants. It is absolute clarity of vision. For

> ...[t]o enter the world is to be shrouded by a veil, so the spirit can no longer see its former abode, which is heaven. The task of the human spirit on earth is to make the veil transparent, so the spirit can gaze clearly at heaven. (*Mesnevi* IV, 3633-5)

Indeed,

> [p]hysical birth is release from the prison of the womb into the freedom of the world. [And so, too,] [s]piritual birth is release from the prison of the senses into the freedom of God. (*Mesnevi* III, 3574-6)

The processes of spiritual and physical birth are mirror images of each other, but the second birth, the spiritual birth which is a release of the soul from its sensual, sensible fetters, is the ultimate goal of the mystic.[60]

---

[60] We can certainly recognize a Socratic tone to such a series of assertions. Socrates eagerly meets his impending death in the jail cell of the *Phaedo* where he begins his discourse by considering the paradoxic relationship between physical pain and pleasure and ends by reminding Phaedo to offer a cock to Asclepius—the god of heal-

Moreover,

> When you have a direct encounter with God, do not look to the
> sciences to assure you that your encounter is genuine. In fact, once
> you have perceived the beauty of God, the sciences lose their fasci-
> nation… Knowledge of the sciences is like ready cash, which can
> give immediate benefits in the world. The effort required to attain
> spiritual vision is like paying a debt owed to the next world. (*Mesnevi*
> III, 3856-9)

So the sort of knowledge that one gains from science—the knowledge of how the world works in the here and now—and the method
of acquiring such knowledge falls short of the sort of true, spiritual
knowledge—*ma'rifa*—that the mystic hopes to achieve.

And yet, while "real value comes with madness," as the poet writes
in his *Divani Shamsi Tabriz*, he completes that thought regarding real
value and madness with the observation, "majdhub below, scientist
above," suggesting that he retains a profound respect for what science
has to offer. This is perhaps cognate with his discussions of the importance of nature, even as he looks beyond nature for the ultimate Reality, the innermost recesses of which he seeks.

Or we might understand it this way: *"majdhub"* is a term that
refers to one who has become ecstatic—who has stepped outside him/
herself into intimacy with the *mysterion*—in holy enlightenment. So the
pursuer of *profanus* knowledge—the scientist—is, in some way, in being
above, valued even more than the ecstatic mystic. But of course it is
not that simple: the poem (*Divani Shamsi Tabriz* #1249) often juxta-
posed with this couplet asserts:

> I have lived on the lip
> of insanity, wanting to know reasons,
> knocking on a door. It opens.
> I've been knocking on the inside!

---

ing—on his behalf, now that he will be freed of the demands of his body and able
to enquire more effectively into truth. (I mention this parallel in anticipation of the
way in which Gülen will be seen to encompass such parallel threads of Socratic/
Platonic thought within the web of his own thinking).

—which offers a gloss on madness, *ma'rifa*, science and rationality when followed by (or preceded by, or merely considered together with) the couplet:

> Real value comes from madness,
> *majdhub* below, scientist above.

For if what appeared to be the outside (he was knocking on the door, of course, from what appeared to be the outside—why else would he be knocking to try to get in?) but the poet realized he had been on the inside all along when it opened—or that "outside" and "inside" are *profanus* concepts that don't apply when one engages the *sacer* (especially the *mysterion* within the *sacer*). So, like "outside" and "inside," "above" and "below" must also be understood to be questionable with regard to their spatially relative meaning.[61] If in the *profanus*, the scientist is above, when one interfaces with the *sacer*, neither the *majdhub* nor the scientist is above—*or* below.

Neither of them is above the other, for Rumi does not unequivocally discount the importance of the physical world. As the outcome of the Divine creative process, in which God is found within all the nooks and crannies of the world, the poet's panhenotheistic sensibilities could not do otherwise than to recognize the validity of everything tangible around us:

> If inner workings were all that mattered, God would not have bothered to create the world. If loving God were purely a spiritual state requiring no outward expression, God would not have bothered to create the world. Just as lovers express their love through material tokens, God expresses His love through creation – and we must express our love for Him by the way we use His creation. (*Mesnevi* I, 2624-7)

Indeed, he sees nature reflected in the very physical process that characterizes the *dhikr* of his followers, the whirling, Mevlevi dervishes—and see them reflected in nature:

---

[61] We recall, too, how al-Qushairi, in discussing al-Hallaj's discussion of God, refers to the irrelevance of "above" and "below" for God.

...Tree limbs rise and fall like ecstatic arms
Of those who have submitted to the mystical life.

(Mesnevi IV, 3264)

The macrocosm of the outer world and the inner process of remembering and seeking oneness with the Source of all worlds are analogues of each other. More to the point:

... There's a strange frenzy in my head,
Of birds flying.
Each particle circulating on its own.
Is the one I love *everywhere*?

(Divani Shamsi Tabriz, #2597)

But the endpoint of this rhetorical question is the realization that the *actualization* of the importance of the world, as opposed to its *potential* importance, is achieved when humans operate in a responsible manner toward it. We emulate God, who, out of love, created the world and loves the world that He created, when we behave with love toward the world—which is in turn a means of expressing our love for God.

The mystic seeks the innermost, hiddenmost recesses of God, but because God is everywhere within the world, and above all embedded in all humans as the apogee of the creation, then seeking God and loving God may be accomplished when we are most fully human, and we are most fully human—we most effectively fulfill God's Will for us—when we seek oneness with God by acting responsibly and lovingly toward the world. This makes manifest God's spirit, since God's spirit is within our own and our own is within God—as becomes clear when we operate responsibly:

By expressing our own inner spirit, we are making manifest the hidden spirit of God. In this way we fulfill God's purpose for us on earth. *(Mesnevi* V, 247)

For

God created us in his own image. To describe God is to describe perfect humanity. *(Mesnevi* IV, 1194)

Part of the paradox that the mystical experience solves, when it succeeds—in Sufism, this notion goes back to Rabi'a, the late 8th-century figure briefly referenced in the preceding chapter, who was instrumental in bringing the imagery of love into the discussion of the mystical quest—is that the mystic seeking God's *mysterion*, as a lover seeks his beloved, is in fact the beloved sought *by* God, the ultimate and eternal lover:

> A lover seeks his beloved; but he also wants his beloved to seek him. God seeks every human being, but He also wants human beings to seek Him. (*Mesnevi* III 4393-4)

Thusly motivated, the lover/mystic seeks, and as Rumi expresses it, succeeds in solving what has been called "the seducer's paradox." For the seducer wishes to contrive a situation in which the one he desires ends up desiring him: the one he wishes to seduce ends up seducing him. When the mystic seeks God's innermost core God has succeeded in solving that seducer's paradox, turning His beloved into a lover and Himself, the ultimate Lover, into the Beloved. Rumi makes frequent use of the imagery of love to describe the relationship between God and the mystic:

> When you are a lover, you want your beloved to be a lover also. God is humanity's greatest lover; and we, His beloved, must become His lovers. (*Mesnevi* I 1736)

Moreover, as "[t]he thirsty seek water, …water also seeks the thirsty" (*Mesnevi* I, 1741). We are the thirsty who thirst for God, but God as the water seeks us—as God thirsts for us who, as water, seek God. For

> [d]esire for God leads us to want to know God. Knowledge of God causes us to love Him. It is impossible to love God if you have a false conception of Him. But those who possess true knowledge of God cannot help loving Him. (*Mesnevi* II, 1532-4)

To get there—to arrive at a condition of knowing God, which is to be filled with God—one must empty one's self of one's *self*:

... The poet has said
that a true seeker must be completely empty like a lute
to make the sweet music of *Lord, Lord*...

(*Mesnevi* VI, 4210)

But love and the emptying of one's self of self in order to be truly immersed in love always have their dangers: to love is to die—the "you" who you were before being in love dies—and to be reborn, as the new "you," the one who is in love. To love is, in a fundamental way, to merge your being into someone else's being: to be lost in that other's eyes, as the poets are wont to say, so deeply lost that one can hardly distinguish one from that other—and one sees the world, as it were, through one's lover's eyes. The danger is that one so loses one's self that one cannot refind that self, and functioning in the world is then difficult. How much the more so if the beloved is God, and one loses one's self within the depths of God's *mysterion*:

> In loving God, you are allowing your own self to be destroyed. In the presence of God you will be reduced to a mere shadow. (*Mesnevi* III, 4622-3)

And again:

> To become holy, you must die to self, and live for the Lord. Only then are the mysteries of God constantly on your lips. To die to self requires great self-discipline, in which you endure great physical and emotional pain. (*Mesnevi* III, 3364-5)

The common-parlance danger for the mystic of loving God so intensely was well exemplified, in the everyday sense, by the fate of Hallaj, as we have earlier noted, who was so caught up in God and God in him that, emerging from his state of ecstasy, with the "mysteries of God [still] constantly on [his] lips," he cried out with his statement, *Ana al'haqq*, that led to his execution as an apostate. Of course, on the other hand, because he was no everyday being immersed in an everyday, common-parlance ecstatic experience, Hallaj *embraced* his execution as a means of returning him to that Other Realm that he had tasted in his passionate embrace of the *mysterion*. Rumi wraps Hallaj within the expression of God and the beauty of nature as articulated in the blood-red of passion shared by a ruby and a sunrise—God and the mystic, the mystic and God—contained without confinement within the blood-red passion of the lover and the beloved:

> …She asks: "Do you love me or yourself more?
> Really, tell the absolute truth."
>
> He says, "There's nothing left of *me*.
> I'm like a ruby held up to the sunrise.
> Is it still a stone, or a world
> made of redness? It has no resistance
> to sunlight.
>
> This is how Hallaj said, *I am the Truth*,
> and told the truth!
>
> The ruby and the sunrise are one… (*Mesnevi* V, 2020 ff)

The fact is—as Rumi writes elsewhere—that Hallaj attained that perfect union and *wanted* to return to the reality beyond reality, the innermost core of the *Being* beyond all being:

> …Hallaj said, *I am the Truth*, and lived it out.
> What happens when the *I* disappears?
> What's left after *not*? (*Mesnevi* VI, 2075)

The fact is that the words to describe that *not* are impossible to come by in our reality, and Hallaj, who experienced it, could not express it, so his words were mistaken for apostasy.

The fact is that the process of seeking and of gaining the goal of oneness with the One Ultimate Being that is beyond the furthest star and yet buried within each of ourselves is simultaneously predicated on an emptying and arrives at an emptying and predicated on being filled with pure being and arrives at fullness. Rumi writes, in his lover's dialect, as his entire being is arrested by God's beauty, that

> … I saw you and became empty.
> This emptiness, more beautiful than existence,
> it obliterated existence, and yet when it comes,
> existence thrives and creates more existence!
>
> (*Divani Shamsi Tabriz* #940)

But he also writes, in that same dialect, as his soul experiences the *rida* (satisfaction) of *mahabba* (love) and of *fana'* (complete annihilation), that derives from and arrives at absolute *tawakkul* (trust) in the Beloved who is God, that

> I am filled with You.
> Skin, blood, bone, brain, and soul.
> There's no room for lack of trust, or trust.
> Nothing in this existence but that existence.
>
> (*Divani Shamsi Tabriz* #168)

The fact is that the goal of losing one's self is not only a marvelous goal with respect to merging with the *mysterion*, but with respect to improving the world by eliminating the self-centeredness that otherwise prevents us from maximizing our efforts on behalf of others, for "[t]he sense of self is like an intoxicating wine. It removes intellect from the head and modesty from the heart" (V 1920). And if we can eliminate that wine, our intellect and our modesty are enhanced and our role in improving the world—in partnering with God to help it achieve (or re-achieve) perfection—is enlarged.

> One day a woman asked her lover, "do you love me more than you love yourself?" He replied, "I love you so much that I am full of you from head to toe. There is no distinction between loving you and loving myself; loving myself is loving you." If you love God, you will feel towards Him as that lover feels towards his beloved. (*Mesnevi* V, 2020-24)

And again—in the very preface to Book II of the *Mesnevi*—he asserts that

> ... Love has no calculating in it. That's why it's said to be a quality of God and not of human beings. "God loves you" is the only possible sentence. The subject becomes the object so totally that it can't be turned around. Who will the "you" pronoun stand for, if you say "You love God"?

Because, in the end, when and if the mystic has found and merged with the *mysterion*, then

> ... How can a lover be anything but the beloved?

Both the larger role of God in being present and yet not tangible and the matter of how that presence is analogous to the presence of love for those in love is expressed:

> We know the sun exists, but we can never see and understand it because our eyes cannot bear to look directly at it.... The sun alone explains the sun; love alone can explain love. (*Mesnevi* I, 115-16)

* * * * *

Rumi covers a range of different issues in both the prose prayers placed at the outset of each of the six books of the *Mesnevi* and the poetry that follows those invocations. He addresses the problematic at the heart of every religious tradition, due to the inherent and inevitable understanding of God as the ultimate Other (even if—to make things still more complicated—God is other than Other, in being part of us and within us, at least in the Abrahamic traditions): how can we *know* God as we know the elements of our own reality? Thus:

> God hid Himself so that people would have to strive hard to find Him... We know joy by its opposite, suffering; we know light by its opposite, darkness. But God has no opposite; either we perceive Him with the eyes of the spirit, or we are spiritually blind. (*Mesnevi* I, 1130-36)

Thus the answer to the question is, in its way, as simple as the question is unbearably complex: we can know God only through faith which is of a different order from the knowledge we possess or seek to possess of our own reality. But the starting point of that simple answer is the realization that we must abandon the methodologies relevant to our own reality, in which we understand everything as relative to its opposite—for God and God's reality won't conform to that paradigm. God offers His own unique paradigm: an Absolute Light that has no opposing darkness by which to recognize it as light.

On the other hand, part of how we know God is by improving the reality around us which God created—so that God is to be found all around us and within us and not only beyond us—which, by further paradox, requires our effort to perfect it, in partnership with God:

"The task of life is to bring harmony between opposites" (*Mesnevi* I, 1293). To the extent that we succeed in turning opposites into parts of harmonious wholes rather than allowing them to persist as antagonistic opposites, we are part of the process of perfecting the world—of completing the process of turning what began as no-thingness and as chaos into a perfect order. Or put otherwise, to turn the world in which we dwell into the Eden inhabited by our aboriginal ancestors and from which they were pushed out for resisting and abrogating God's explicit command.

Indeed, he constantly writes about the matter of harmonizing, not just among the various elements of our world that appear to be opposed, but in balancing between an appreciation for our material world and at the same time a recognition that there is not only another reality beyond our own, but that it is, in a fundamental way, a purer, more desirable reality with which to be in contact. This is, of course, what we might expect of a mystic, whose focus is profoundly directed toward that other reality, and who seeks within it for its innermost, hiddenmost core. But Rumi, as much as he is the consummate mystic, does not seek to simply move beyond our reality to that other and its hidden core—because to do so would be to fail to recognize that the Creator is found not only *beyond* our reality but embedded *within* it—that the Creator is to be found within the creation and not only beyond it.

Harmony, as that term is first used by the Hellenistic Greek musicologist, Aristoxenus, refers to the meeting of two opposed tones to yield a mellifluous result.[62] That usage is derived from the larger notion of combining opposite ideas—ideas that don't necessarily seem to work logically together. This sense of harmony shapes part of the heart of Rumi's thought.

For Rumi, the ultimate paradox is God, as God is for every mystic. The all-powerful, all-good, perfect God has engendered a universe that is not perfect, in which evil manifestly exists, no part of which is

---

[62] For details on Aristoxenus' Harmonics, see Henry S. Macran, ed. and transl., *The Harmonics of Aristoxenus*. Oxford: Clarendon Press, 1902, especially 224 (note to 95.5).

devoid of powerlessness, provoking the obvious question: how can it exist? How did it come into being? In the general division within Muslim theological thinking between the Mu'tazilites and the Ash'arites, the first group notes that evil cannot have come into being through God's creative energy, because that would contradict what God is as an all-good being. But the second group observes that to deny God the possibility for having engendered evil would be to limit God's all-powerful capacity. Rumi solves the paradox when he asserts that

> Since bad things too come from Him, you feel doubt,
>   His grace can have no flaws; pure throughout
> Giving bad things is part of His perfection,
>   Just listen to this tale which aids reflection
> A painter painted two works on a wall
>   One stunning and one with no worth at all:
> He painted houris and fair Joseph's face,
>   Then demons' heads in the remaining space
> Both types of forms show His intelligence;
>   It is not His ugliness, but eminence
> He makes the vile as ugly as can be-
>   All ugliness surrounds them totally-
> To manifest His knowledge's perfect;
>   Deniers of this fact must face rejection.
> Don't claim he can't make ugliness as well!
> He makes the faithful and the infidel.[63]

Thus the Sufi, who seeks the *mysterion* within the paradoxical God must himself be buried in paradox to find what he seeks, beginning with his experience in the here and now. Therefore,

> ...[s]omeone once asked a great shaikh
> What Sufism was.
> "The feeling of joy
> When sudden disappointment comes,"
>
> (*Mesnevi* III, 3260)

was the shaikh's response.

---

[63] Rumi, *The Masnavi*, Book Two, A New Translation by Jawid Mojaddedi, New York: Oxford University Press, 2008, p. 148.

But this does not mean that the imperfect universe cannot be per-
fected. On the contrary, it is in the process of becoming perfect, coming closer and closer to the perfect God that created it. It simply takes
time:

> ... Initially you conceive a tall tree in your garden; then you con-
> sider where best to obtain a sapling. But planting the sapling occurs
> many years before you possess a tall tree in your garden. Long ago
> God conceived a glorious, harmonious universe, and then consid-
> ered how to create it. He planted the universe; but it has not yet
> realized its purpose. (*Mesnevi* II, 972-4)

So there is a purpose even to evil in the world—it is part of God's
ongoing desire to instruct us, who are so far from being perfect. Since
we cannot conceive of absolute beauty or absolute good due to the
limits of our vision, then we need ugliness and even evil in order to
gain perspective, to begin to think of relative beauty and good and to
use that relative awareness as a means of striving to grasp absolute beauty and good—which is the process in which the mystic engages. Rumi
states the paradox even more concisely:

> Since truth and falsehood are mixed together in this world, God
> reveals Himself and hides Himself in the same events. (*Mesnevi* II,
> 2966-7)

And if, as is so often asserted among the Abrahamic traditions,
evil enters the world through human disobedience to God's com-
mandments—and this, in turn, is facilitated by God Who gifts us with
free will (which gift we then immediately abuse as Adam and Eve dis-
obey God at the outset of human reality), yet we are reminded that
the overriding feature of that gift is that it is a good gift, from God,
and that even as it is misused by us, that there is a purpose to it. For
without free will, our relationship to God would be simply that of
soulless robots.

> God's Will has given rise to our free will. His Will is invisible beneath
> the dust; ours is visible. His Will creates our free will. When He
> gives a command, He does not compel obedience, but invites it.
> (*Mesnevi* V, 3087-8)

Rumi seeks the place in which to respond to that invitation—a place beyond place within his soul, which is a place in which God and all mystics meet. There,

> Out beyond ideas of wrongdoing and right doing,
> There is a field. I'll meet you there.

It is a place where,

> When the soul lies down in that grass,
> The world is too full to talk about.
> Ideas, language, even the phrase *each other*
> Doesn't make any sense.
>
> (*Divani Shamsi Tabriz* #158)

For it is a place where all the seekers, all the lovers of God, the Beloved, the Sought-after One, converge as one with the One, regardless of the point and tradition from which any of them began.

It is a place where Fethullah Gülen has settled over the decades, as he simultaneously yearns toward the *mysterion* and applies that yearning to inspiring action in the world of the here and now in order to serve God in perfecting it—as we shall consider in the chapters that follow.

Chapter Three

Biographical Contexts:
The Intellectual Shaping of Fethullah Gülen

There is any number of features that one could consider in discussing the world into which Fethullah Gülen was born, and the historical backdrop that led to the shaping of that world. For nearly six centuries—from the early fourteenth century through the end of World War I—the Ottoman Empire had dominated parts or nearly all of the Middle East; through much of that time the Empire had extended into Europe, conquering as far as the edge of Vienna in 1529 and again in 1683. For the purposes of our discussion, there is a particular series of issues that are relevant.

As a Muslim state the empire embraced and operated according to certain principles vis-à-vis non-Muslim inhabitants of its domains. Specifically, groups such as Jews, Christians, Zoroastrians and others whose form of faith was centered on a text were classified as *dhimmi*—"people of the pact." That pact—*dhimma*—is traditionally understood to have originated in a contract arrived at between the Prophet Muhammad and the Jewish Banu Nadir tribe and their allies in 628. In that year, leaving Yathrib (later known as al-Madina—"the City"—due to its importance in the life of Muhammad and the shaping of Islam) to establish his control over the *hijaz*, with Makka as the political (and future religious) center of the region, Muhammad passed 150 kilometers from his base toward the oasis town of Khaybar, where the Banu Nadir had come to dwell. His forces besieged Khaybar for 30 days.

In capitulating to Muhammad the Banu Nadir tribe agreed to a pact which is said to have offered them untrammeled rights to continue to worship as Jews in exchange for half of their produce as a negotiated *jizya*—a head tax. We have no written record of this agreement. What survives from the early centuries of Muslim history is a pact associated with Umar—and it is not absolutely clear as to whether the Umar so-referenced is one of the Prophet's early companions and followers, (the second rightly-guided caliph after Abu Bakr), or Umar II, a caliph from about 720ff.[64]

These questions pertaining to the precise shape of the early *dhimma* become significant as we follow through the centuries leading to our own time. There are in any case at least three aspects of the *dhimma* issue that are relevant to our discussion. The first is that, whereas the earliest such contract apparently applied, as I have suggested, to the relations between Muslims and Jews, sooner than later it came to apply to any and all groups whose relationship with divinity is mediated by a divinely-inspired text: the peoples of the pact are diverse peoples (notably: Jews, Christians, Zoroastrians and Sabaeans) of the book.

The second issue of interest is that, over the long time and wide place under Muslim governance throughout the centuries the sense of exactly how the conditions of *dhimma* should be carried out has varied. Historically, places under Muslim control have tended to be considerably more generous with their non-Muslim inhabitants than, say, places under Christian control have been vis-à-vis non-Christian inhabitants. Perhaps the most extreme instance of this may be seen in August, 1492, when Jews were summarily exiled from a newly unified Christian Spain after having resided there for perhaps 14 centuries; they were offered refuge and support within the realm of the Ottomans.

There were exceptions to this rule (such as the Almohad persecution of *dhimmi* in the years following the Almohad conquest of Cordoba in 1148), and through the six centuries of Ottoman rule there were higher times and lower times for *dhimmi*—and by and large there were

---

[64] The form in which the *dhimma* is articulated is as reported, regarding the dialogue between 'Umar and a *Christian* (not Jewish) community, perhaps in Syria, by 'Abd al-Rahman b. Ghanam (d. 697), but it is recorded in writing later.

limits to how high a *dhimmi* could aspire—but the times and places where Jews or Muslims could flourish within Christendom before the late nineteenth century were much fewer and farther between by comparison.

The third aspect of this issue raises questions for the future as much as it does for the past. That is: to what extent do Muslim authorities view the *dhimma* as ordained by God? If Muhammad established the first *dhimma* does that mean that the act is divinely sanctioned, even if there is no mention of it in God's own words in the Qur'an? If the earliest version of the *dhimma* dates from well after Muhammad—be it the time of Umar I or that of Umar II—how binding are its precepts to a Muslim leader? What are the implications for the notion of an even playing field for Muslims and non-Muslims in an Islamic state?

As it turns out, we have one possible answer within the Ottoman Turkish Empire of the last few generations before World War I and the collapse of that state. A *firman* (decree) by Sultan Abdulmecid I in 1856 eliminated entirely the idea of a *dhimma* throughout his realm. That decree was confirmed by his successors—so as a practical historical matter one may say of the *dhimma* idea that it ceased to exist during the last several generations of Ottoman rule. Of course, when in the aftermath of the collapse of the regime Kemal Atatürk managed to establish the modern state of Turkey he altogether eliminated religion as an aspect of administering the state.

If on the one hand and at first glance Atatürk's shaping of the state may be understood as a logical furthering of the late Ottoman policies that eliminated the *dhimma* concept, on the other hand, there were those who felt that pure secularization deprived Turkey of a substantial component of its identity. Based on a long history as a Muslim country, how could or would the modern state of Turkey function in ignoring that aspect of its very soul? Moreover, whereas Atatürk seems to have feared that the persistence of an official Islamic identity would doom the state to backwardness, unable to compete in a modern world in which the sciences were so important to progress, there were those who argued strenuously that, both historically and conceptually, there was no inconsistency between Islam and the sciences, that in fact properly understood and interpreted, Islam and science are entirely compatible.

Atatürk's secularist regime proved more than a little bit oppressive to those who championed an Islamic perspective, and blind to the possibilities proposed by Islamic thinkers who sought to express the ways in which the religious traditions laid down by the Prophet and his successors were hospitable to modern scientific thinking. Among such individuals, one who stood out was Bediüzzaman Said Nursi (1878–1960), an extraordinary Turkish scholar of Islam who argued that Muslims should embrace the benefits available in modernity and seek to connect those benefits to the content of Islam's sacred texts by studying them with a mind to their engagement of ideas and accomplishments that are part of the modern world.[65]

As a child, Nursi was already recognized as having a prodigious memory and, emerging into adulthood he supplemented a traditional Islamic education centered in the *madrasah* and its study of the Qur'an, Hadith and Islamic jurisprudence—an education he completed by the age of 14—with studies in philosophy, mathematics and the physical sciences. He also grew up during the waning decades of the Ottoman regime and lived through its final collapse during and after World War I and the emergence of the modern state under the leadership of Atatürk. Most of the first twenty-five years of the Republic were marked by a militarist sort of rule that, in its assertive secularist mood tended to oppress thinkers like Nursi who promoted an interest in traditional spiritual matters.

Nursi appreciated the importance of *madrasah*-based learning and found it in but of itself inadequate for those desirous of having a positive effect on their families, communities and indeed the world. At the very time when the Ottoman regime was moving toward its demise, he was shaping a new educational program—a blueprint for a broadly conceived university, the *Medrestu'z Zehra* (Resplendent *Madrasah*)

---

[65] Indeed, "Bediüzzaman" is not a name given to him by his parents at birth, but an honorific, bestowed on him later, and meaning "The Wonder of the Age," referring to the extraordinary breadth and depth of his scholarship at a young age.

within Turkey's eastern provinces. In 1907 he travelled to Istanbul, where Sultan Abdulhamid II—the year before he was overthrown by the "Young Turks"—received him and offered financial support for the founding of such a university. In spite of the overthrow of the Sultan in 1908, foundations were laid by 1913—but the advent of the War the following year and the events that followed prevented the realization of this project.

The war, for better and for worse, was diversely fruitful for Nursi. During the first two years he composed his first series of commentaries on the Qur'an—commentaries that had as their primary goal to demonstrate the compatibility of the Qur'an with contemporary science. He is said to have done this while in the saddle, dictating the words to associates that would evolve into his most renowned work, *Risale-i Nur*. But the war context that inspired such commentaries also further broadened Nursi's experience of the world beyond where books had taken him.

What he dictated he did while serving in the military, commanding forces on the Caucasian Front against the Russians—he was taken prisoner in March, 1916 and was not able to escape until early 1918, after which he returned to Istanbul by way of Warsaw, Berlin and Vienna—for which he was later awarded a War Medal from the Ottoman Ministry of War. But it was the struggle for a new state to come into being in the aftermath of the war and the collapse of the old regime—the battles both within Turkish society and between Turkey and the primary World War I victors, the British and the French, with their vision of political domination of the entire Middle Eastern region— that gradually pulled Nursi away from interest and involvement in public life.

On the one hand, his reputation in the aftermath of his war heroism was significant enough so that Mustafa Kemal, the eventual leader of the victory against the British and the French, not only recognized it. He invited Nursi to come to Ankara, to participate in the process of thinking out how, precisely, to shape the new state of Turkey. On the other hand, his sense of disillusionment with the political world and the world of the here and now—his increasing sense of the limits of human capabilities, vast though those capabilities may be—led him increasingly to look inward, to pursue his own spiritual training. Moreover, in the course of spending nearly eight months in the Turkish capital as part of the group founding the state, he understood that the military elite led by Atatürk—the maturing group of once-young Turkish officers who had deposed Abdulhamid II in 1908—sought to shape a secular republic in which Islam was to be actively ignored.

Although he was offered various posts in the new administration, he declined, retiring instead to Van in eastern Turkey, where he focused on spiritual practices and lived largely in isolation. Oddly, he was arrested in 1925 and charged with having taken part in an uprising in the eastern provinces against the government although there is no evidence at all that he had—or that he was even interested in being involved in political matters at that point. He was exiled into western Anatolia along with many others.

It was during this period of oppression and deprivation that, in a remote village in the mountains in the Isparta province—the village of Barla—Nursi resumed his work on the *Risale-i Nur* (*Message of Light*).[66] This extensive collection—it ultimately came to over 6,000 pages—of informally structured Qur'anic commentaries (*tafsir*) diverged from the traditional direction of *tafsir*, not only in its structure (and it was being conceived not in the quiet of the study but on foot, so to speak) but also in that it focused on establishing connections between the sacred text and the contemporary natural and scientific world around us. Nursi had spent a good deal of time studying the natural sciences, even while he studied the Qur'an and Islamic jurisprudence and theology. Interestingly, this continued work—like earlier material, dictated rapidly in Nursi's places of exile—was distributed in copies printed by hand and distributed in secret, because the secularist regime had forbidden the circulation of religious works. It was also not written

---

[66] Note that the word *"risala"* (which is also used, as we have seen, as the title of works such as that by al-Qushairi) derives from the same root as the word *"rasul,"* which latter term is used to refer to only a handful of prophetic figures in the Muslim tradition, most obviously, Muhammad.

out in the Latin letters adopted for Turkey by the Atatürk administration until 1956.[67]

What resulted, it is said, is that some 600,000 hand-written copies of Nursi's work were ultimately circulated around the country. As such, Nursi, who had no political ambitions, became in exile the de facto founder of a movement known as the Nur movement (*Nur hareketi*). The movement, centered on Nursi's thinking and writing, is emblematic in particular of the discussion of religion—specifically Islam—and science that was conducted in Turkey, interwoven with the interweave between socio-political life and religion that is endemic to human history, during the first half of the twentieth century.

Moreover, as the Nur movement spread into the 1950s in spite of extensive efforts on the part of the state administration to crush it, it found new adherents in the generation of Turks who, in their youths had passed through state-run, highly secularized educational institutions. In other words, the concerted attempt to eliminate spirituality from the identity of the Turkish people may be said to have back-fired, in part at least, in that the yearning for something beyond what secular science and society have to offer drove many young people into the arms of the Nur movement. By the end of the 1950s, in the last years before his death, Nursi's influence spread beyond Turkey itself.

Arguably, the essence of Nursi's thinking was the synthesis between the thought expressed in the Qur'an and hadith and that in contem-

---

[67] The Ottoman Empire had adopted Arabic centuries earlier as its writing vehicle. But as a practical phonemic-linguistic matter, Arabic as a language emphasizes consonants and minimizes vowel contrasts, (and in fact is usually written altogether without vowels), whereas Turkish is emphatic in its use of vowel coloration, so that Arabic offers an awkward means of conveying the phonology of Turkish in written form. Ataturk's desire to modernize the new republic included the change in 1928-9 to a writing system more conducive to conducting the business of the state and educating its populace. For someone like Nursi, the change was symbolic of a policy of throwing out the baby with the bath-water, especially since, as a Muslim entity, the Ottoman state also had typically used the Arabic language and not merely its writing system for matters pertaining to religion (as it most often used Persian for matters pertaining to art and culture). The continued use of the Arabic writing system by his followers was in part a statement of their desire not to abandon positive elements of the late Ottoman-era administration, especially its spiritual elements.

porary physical sciences, in both of which areas he was well-versed. Rather than perceiving dissonance between the two strains of thought in their respective relationship to reality, Nursi saw in the Qur'an passages and ideas that presage and are consonant with modern scientific discovery. Thus, for instance, instead of rejecting the Newtonian worldview as antithetical to the cosmological perspective of traditional Islam in both its juridical and its more mystical aspects, he re-visioned Newtonian dynamics through an argument from-design set of lenses.

For example, the Qur'anic "Light verse" (*Ayat an-Nur*; 24:35) is said by Nursi to allude to the eventual discovery and development of electricity; and a verse fragment such as "...*We have created for them similar [vessels] on which they ride*" (Qur'an 36:42) is taken to anticipate the development of the railroad system. "*To Solomon [We made] the wind obedient: its early morning [stride] was a month's journey, and its evening [stride] was a month's journey...*" (Qur'an 34:12) is connected to the eventual creation of airplanes—indeed, it "points far ahead of today's airplanes."[68] There are many other passages of this type that establish a correspondence between Qur'anic verses and twentieth-century scientific findings. This notion of decoding the language of the sacred text toward anticipating and understanding the decoding of nature's hidden texts had a profound influence on the many who followed his writings.

One of the obvious distinctions between Nursi's formulation and its earlier religious—Sufi and non-Sufi—siblings is the context in which he shaped his: one of operating within an environment of state-sponsored persecution. As a practical matter, the process of shaping his ideas took place under duress and through hasty dictation to others, as opposed to being accomplished in a systematic manner under calm academic or other circumstances. His work, to repeat, was copied again and again by hand and distributed clandestinely. Moreover, some of his stu-

---

[68] Bediüzzaman Said Nursi, *The Words* (*Sözler*). (Istanbul: Sözler Neşriyat, 1998), 806. This is the first of the four major sections of the *Risale-i Nur*. The others are "The Letters" (*Mektubat*), "The Flashes' (*Lem'alar*) and "The Rays" (*Şualar*). Smaller sections and pamphlets (for example, "The Damascus Sermon") further may be seen to extend it to its full form.

dents were so determined to pursue his line of thinking that virtually anything new within the world of science was said by them to be hinted at in the verses of the Qur'an. But Nursi's wide following was in part a function of the reality that there were many young people seeking spiritual nourishment in a society that, in approaching religion with a frontal attack, offered no nourishment at all.

In articulating God as the supreme Craftsman—the Divine Artisan—Nursi embraced a mechanistic understanding that both points to its Maker and embraces a teleological view. He thus shaped a distinctly Islamic version of the late-eighteenth and nineteenth-century deist viewpoint that saw the universe as a splendidly wound-up clock, a working machine that continues to function into infinite time. For Nursi was clear that the Prime Mover behind the universe is the Self-Subsisting God whose continuous presence, purposes and interest in the world are attested in the sacred texts of various traditions, culminating with the Qur'an.

* * * * *

Among those who were drawn to the sort of thinking exemplified by Bediüzzaman Said Nursi was Fethullah Gülen. The world into which Gülen was born in 1941 was one where, in his country of birth, the Ottoman reality with a staunchly proclaimed declaration of complete religious freedom had been succeeded by a secular republic in which religion would play absolutely no role within the administration of the state and religious practice was suppressed in the public sphere. Growing up in such an atmosphere, but training to become an imam, Gülen surely wondered whether the course taken by Atatürk was leading in the right direction. And, as we shall see, the thinking of Said Nursi would provide a starting point from which Gülen would go still further in terms of the content of his own writings, the activist direction those writings would inspire, and the far-flung nature of his influence—while, like Nursi, Gülen never opposed the laws. Indeed, Gülen's role as an educator, from the beginning to the present, is rooted very much within a framework consistent with government policies, as we shall see.

Fethullah Gülen was born in Erzurum into a family of limited means. His father was an imam who spent much of his time reading and reflecting on the shape of the early Islamic world. He enjoyed reciting poetry and was an important early inspirer of his son, both as a lover of learning and as one impassioned with the stories and teachings of Muhammad and his Companions. So, too, Gülen's mother, a teacher of Qur'an, instilled in him a love of recitation from that sacred text. Indeed it was she who began to teach him how to recite the Qur'an when he was four years old.

Gülen was educated along traditional Islamic lines—he became a *hafiz*, one who knows the entire Qur'an by heart, by age twelve; and he began to preach in local mosques as a fourteen-year-old—and also along modern lines, beginning a life-long series of intellectual and spiritual interests that extend from the Qur'an and hadith to the literatures of other religious traditions to math and the sciences. His study encompassed the history of Islam and its own unique contributions over an extended period of time to math and science—and not only to Abrahamic spirituality.

Aside from his formally obtained, government-mandated, teaching certificate in Islamic learning Gülen became part of the training circles of local Sufi sheikhs, with their focus both on deep—mystical—spirituality and on a universalist, broadly humanistic perspective with regard to faith. On the one hand, a centerpiece of such study that would emerge for him as an interest and an influence was Jalaluddin Rumi, as well as other key Sufi thinkers. On the other hand, his intellectual and spiritual reach would extend as deeply into the Western tradition as Plato and Aristotle, and as far forward as the teachings of Bediüzzaman Said Nursi.

By 1958 Gülen had taken and passed the formal examinations administered by the Turkish State's Directorate of Religious Affairs, thus allowing him to be officially appointed as an imam, preacher and teacher. His first appointment was to a mosque in Edirne, not far from Istanbul, on the European side of Turkey. There he lived modestly—indeed ascetically—as he continued his self-directed course of diverse studies while quickly developing a reputation throughout the city as an outstanding preacher. He developed a web of friends and supporters from varied walks of life through his appealing personality and the breadth and diverse depth of his learning.

This was also the formative period, for him, of perceiving in the contours of Turkish society a diminishment of moral and spiritual values. He developed a concern for the future of youth caught in a matrix of spiritual uncertainty and lack of moral clarity and found himself driven to seek a way to redirect them away from that sense of being lost. After doing his military service he returned to Edirne. He began to reach out by way of a series of public lectures that, together with his preaching within the confines of his mosque, led to his promotion to a new post. First transferred to Kirklareli, in 1966 Gülen became the main preacher and an unpaid teacher in a boarding school in Izmir, Turkey's third-largest city.

The move to Izmir would be transformative to Gülen's life and his career. There, as his own thinking deepened and broadened through ever more diverse self-directed reading, his charismatic influence began to spread through a wide range of preaching and teaching, delivering lectures and leading seminars. He addressed varied subjects, from religious study and practice—focused on the Qur'an and the hadith and their relationship both to Muslim jurisprudence and theology and to the modern world—to education theory and its relationship to shaping children into adults with a concern for others: a devotion to social justice and a passion for appreciating and maintaining the natural world around us.

In Izmir he began to redirect the role of the mosque toward what it had been in Islam's golden age: the center of life, attending not only to the prayer-centered spiritual needs of its constituents, but to their psychological and intellectual needs as well. He did not merely preach Friday sermons, but conducted discussions which focused on the questions relating to everyday life—both their concerns and the issues about which they were merely curious—to which the Muslim tradition, linked to contemporary thought, offers answers. His deep learning and his psychological acuity combined to help him develop a reputation and to expand his following.

At the same time, over the next several years he began with greater and greater clarity to encircle his preaching and the discussions he led with a call to action along lines centered on the concept of serving others: *hizmet* (which is the Turkish term for "service"). Particularly in his devotion to the encouraging of young people to think about the future of the world and their role in shaping it toward a fuller beauty, in his pushing them to recognize the importance of interweaving intellectual awareness with both spiritually-grounded virtue and altruistic service toward others, he helped foster a generation grounded in the conviction that such service in the best of ways serves the self. For he emphasized how each "self" is connected to all "selves" and thus that helping others and helping to improve the world benefits the one helping.

Consider the era: the 1960s, when socio-cultural and political turmoil prevailed across much of the Western world. Turkey, too, was subject to a good deal of political turmoil and, as elsewhere in the world, young people were often drawn to extremist ideologies perceived as pure. In many cases extremism also meant turning to violence. Against such a backdrop, Gülen preached and discussed at a feverish pace in his desire to inspire Turkish youth to act toward shaping a peaceful world, not a violent one, fraught not with ego-centric politics but with service to society at large.

With this ambition in mind, Gülen travelled widely in the years that followed, visiting countless cities and towns and villages across Turkey, giving sermons in mosques and speeches and lectures in coffee-houses and lecture halls. Talks became dialogues, speaking never outpaced listening, as he sought both the pulse of the Turkish people and a means of influencing that pulse toward a calmer, more *hizmet*-driven beat. His words were recorded by volunteers and distributed on tape; by the end of the decade he was one of a handful of imams recognized throughout the country.

But his recognizability didn't simply mean that people knew his name. It meant that his charismatic leadership of an ever-growing group of admirers could permit him to influence that group to turn their admiration for him into actions benefiting the community. Thus his encouragement toward developing more effective educational facilities and making education more accessible and available to more young people, including those without the means to pursue their education, led to the building of institutions. It led to the organizing of scholarship-granting entities directed toward economically-deprived students.

It also led, to some extent, to fear of him on the part of the secular government—echoing the condition under which Said Nursi suffered persecution more than a generation earlier. In 1971, Gülen was arrested on false charges that he had been trying to change the Turkish governmental structure toward an Islamicist regime. He remained in prison for several months, eventually released—and later acquitted of the charge.[69] He continued thereafter to teach and to preach, retiring in 1980 from his formal position as an imam.

But by then the number of people inspired by him had expanded exponentially from what it had begun as in the 1960s. Ultimately, by the 1980s, an extensive network of Gülen-inspired groups of educators and entrepreneurs began an extended program of establishing schools—by now, several hundred of them both within and beyond Turkey. Private institutions, these schools offered—and continue to offer—an incomparable opportunity for the students from all walks of life; they abide by the strictures demanded by the state but extend well beyond those strictures to offer well-balanced curricula that wed tradition to modernity and interweave a focus on the intellect with an interest in the soul and a recognition of the importance of the body for those who would become fully contributing members of society.

Indeed the most abiding theme across the panoply of Gülen-inspired schools is that of contributing to society: embrace of the diversity of humanity and *hizmet* on all levels. Over the past decades what might best be called the Gülen, or more correctly, *Hizmet* Movement has extended such an educational initiative not only horizontally outward from Turkey to Turkic countries to the farther and farther reach-

---

[69] Although Gülen has never opposed the government, either by actions or non-actions, he has at times been misunderstood, misinterpreted and perceived as having political ambitions from diverse sides of the political/religious fence.

es of Europe, Asia, Africa and the Americas, but vertically, from school
for young children to colleges and universities.

By 1991 Fethullah Gülen decided that his role as an inspirer of the
Hizmet Movement, through the mechanism of preaching in mosques
and teaching in lecture halls, had gone as far as necessary, or perhaps
as far as it could, as a primary mode of encouraging such actions. He
retired from public life, to devote his time in a quieter way to the
community: to teaching seminars of graduate students and taking
part in service projects. He continued to travel in order to meet with
diverse religious and political world leaders—these would range from
Israel's chief Sephardic Rabbi, Eliyahu Bakshi Doron, to Pope John
Paul II—who share his vision of a better world. He became increasingly available for interviews and commentaries in the various media,
in order to promote the ideas of *Hizmet* and of peaceful coexistence
across the broad range of ethnicities and religions, races and national-
ities that define the spectrum of human society.

He became particularly active in promoting interfaith dialogue—
extracting the most forward-looking of features of Muslim tradition
with regard to embracing non-Muslims and wedding them to contemporary reality. And above all, he expanded the range of his writing projects, thereby making his thinking on both intra-Muslim spiritual matters and on interfaith and multicultural issues available to a
wide audience.

In spite of Gülen's consistent assertion of being apolitical—he has
written and spoken about diverse ideas, from human rights and humane
secularism to democracy, open society and mutual tolerance—as his
renown spread he found himself under fire in effect from two directions. On the one hand, the secular leadership within Turkey feared
that his goal was to eliminate the even playing field among faiths that
evolved during the past 80 years of Turkish history, and to reshape
Turkey as a theocracy. On the other hand, extremist Islamist groups
found his interest and activity in interfaith discussions and initiatives
to be anti-Islamic—accusing him of heresy.

To both sides of this criticism he often repeated the idea that interfaith dialogue and mutual religious respect were both a decisive element

throughout Ottoman Turkish history and in particular in the last generations of that history; and that openness to diverse spiritual perspectives may be understood not merely as acceptable to Islam, but as a Muslim religious *obligation*.[70]

His ultra-secular critics managed to bring criminal charges against him in 2000—which were proven baseless and dismissed eight years later. As a practical matter within the flow of Gülen's personal life, this episode was ultimately irrelevant: he had left Turkey for the United States in 1999 primarily for health reasons—to receive treatment for a cardiovascular condition. This culminated in a heart operation in 2004, and on the advice of his doctors that he avoid stress he has remained in the United States, away from the politically-charged world of Turkey, in a retreat in Pennsylvania where he continues to read and to write and to teach a small group of students and to receive occasional visitors from a range of disciplines and walks of life.

His profound interest in the treble weave—of love of traditional Muslim thought with a passion for contemporary scientific thought; of intra-Islamic concerns with embrace of true interfaith dialogue; and of an insistence that such love, passion, concern and embrace lead one to serve others—marks his most enduring contribution during the past two decades as a writer and activist. It is the relationship between this contribution and that of those who preceded him, particularly Jalaluddin Rumi that will occupy our discussion in the chapters that follow.

---

[70] It might be noted that the opportunities for non-Muslims to achieve high governmental positions have been far fewer under the secular Turkish governments of the past nine decades than was very often the case under the Ottomans during the preceding more than four centuries.

Chapter Four

Gülen's Thought in Its Relation to Rumi and Other Thinkers: Mysticism and the Passion for Interfaith Dialogue

There is a number of particular ways in which one might explore the intellectual and spiritual relationship between the thinking of Jalaluddin Rumi and Fethullah Gülen. The most straightforward starting point, perhaps, would be to summarize the primary themes in Rumi's writings as examined in Chapter II and to consider Gülen's writing as it pertains to the Rumi material and then to consider both where, if at all, Gülen diverges from Rumi and where, related or not to these divergences, Gülen may be seen to relate to other thinkers before or since Rumi's era.

Thus we have noted a number of key themes within Rumi's writing. Among these none is more important to this discussion than his expansion of the universalist theme articulated by Ibn al-'Arabi: that God is focused on and interested in all peoples equally, that the mystic in particular recognizes—or ought to recognize—that access to the *mysterion* may be had from myriad religion-specific directions. As we have seen, Rumi expresses this idea a number of times in a number of ways, both more narrowly and directly, by reference to diverse religious traditions; and more broadly and indirectly, when his panhenotheistic view expands to encompass more, even than humans.

Indeed, sandwiched between different elements of Rumi's universalist and/or panhenotheistic words we have also noted his view of what it is that makes humans different from other species within the creation. "Moses lit up the top of Mount Sinai but the mountain could not hold that light" because the mountain lacks whatever it is that humans possess that caused God to appoint us, according to Qur'an 2:30 as His vice-regents over the earth. That issue leads not only to an understanding of our species as unique but as burdened with a responsibility that the mountain (and the rest of creation) don't have resting on them. It is our obligation, as we noted that Rumi observes, to participate in the ongoing process of perfecting the world, "to bring harmony between opposites" in order ultimately to transform our world into the kind of ideal reality that once defined the Garden of Eden.

We have noted Rumi's sense both of the superiority of the hidden spiritual world over the physical world and of the validity and importance of the physical world—the creation—in which, in the panhenotheistic understanding offered by the poet, God's attributes expressed through His Names are to be found everywhere. Thus just as God is *apart from* our physical reality, God is *a part of* it and accessible through the signs evidenced in His creation. We have seen in Rumi an appreciation of science but a sense of the superiority to it of spirituality in accessing what is of utmost and ultimate importance.

In considering Gülen's thought against this backdrop a number of large issues needs to be kept in mind. One is that his interests and his knowledge are broad and thus we should expect the range of influences on his thinking to be extensive,[71] and obviously not limited to Rumi—this is part of the reason for having expended so much energy in the Introduction and Chapter One of this narrative on an array of figures—although the relationship to Rumi's thought is our primary focus.

A second is that, just as we have not considered everything written by Rumi, we are not encompassing everything written by Gülen. Moreover, in the case of Rumi we have entirely ignored chronology, because the order in which everything was written down is not essential to our discussion. Where Gülen is concerned, the same might be

---

[71] And this narrative by no means presumes to be exhaustive with respect to how many influences upon Gülen from others or connections between Gülen and others may be felt—even within the available constellation of Sufi thinkers, much less beyond that constellation.

said: chronology is not important, unless his views on a given issue significantly change over time. It would seem that they have simply expanded the range of their theoretical and practical applications, rather than changed, per se.

We must also recognize that, just as Rumi is part of a larger Sufi tradition, it would be foolish to try to completely disentangle the similarities between Rumi's thought and Gülen's thought from the relationship between the latter and Sufism at large. These similarities and putative influences are intermingled just as they are interwoven with other influences on Gülen's thought—or other similarities between his thinking and the thinking of others—reflecting the breadth of his intellectual interests.

* * * * *

An obvious starting point for this discussion is love—which, we have observed, enters Sufism as an important principle largely through the efforts of Rabi'a al-'Adawiya in the late 8th century. (Like Rabi'a, Gülen has never married; his spiritual and psychological pre-occupation has been with God and with how to enact God's edifying will with regard to his "family": his students, his community and society, the world at large. There is a number of times and places where Gülen specifically refers to Rabi'a, as when he notes:

> As Rabi'a al-'Adawiya put it, "I swear on Your Holy Being that I have not worshipped You demanding Your Paradise. Rather, I loved You and connected my slavery to my love."... With their hearts they constantly endeavor to stay close to Him, and with their reason and intellect, they observe phenomena in the mirrors of the Divine Names.[72]

He refers to Rabi'a again in an essay focused on the subject, "What It Takes to be a Believer," in which he observes that,

---

[72] "Love of God," in Section One ("Love and Mercy") in M. Fethullah Gülen, *Toward a Global Civilization of Love and Tolerance* (Second Edition). Somerset, NJ: The Light, Inc., 2006, 54.

...In the footsteps of Rabi'a al-'Adawiya they accept everyone and everything as a sweet syrup, even though it may be poison... God loves these people, and they love God... Their wings of humility always rest on the ground...[73]

The theme of love that is adumbrated by Rabi'a is pursued again and again by Gülen, both when he does and when he does not overtly allude to her thought or for that matter to the thought of Rumi, who carried that theme to its apogee as a thinker within the Sufi tradition and who also embraced a world much wider than Sufism or even than Islam in general, as we have seen. Gülen observes:

Love is the most essential element in every being; a most radiant light, a great power that can resist and overcome every force. It elevates every soul that absorbs it...[74]

And again he asserts:

Love of the Creator and yearning for return to Him is the clearest sign of one's being loved by God.[75]

This last statement—of the reciprocal relationship between the mystic seeking God and God seeking the mystic—echoes a panoply of Sufi thinkers. (Gülen alludes to several and to their enhanced capacity for unmitigated love: "The people of love, like Rumi, Yunus, Yesevi, and Bediüzzaman were attached to God at a much greater degree than us, and their fallibility was much less than ours. For this reason, they made tremendous efforts regarding love, affection, and tolerance, and they greatly influenced those around them on this matter....").[76] His state-

---

[73] "What It Takes to be a Believer," in Section Three ("The Ideal Human") of *Love and Tolerance*, 172.

[74] "The Necessity of Interfaith Dialogue," in M. Fethullah Gülen, *Essays—Perspectives—Opinions*, (Somerset, NJ: The Light, 2004 [Second Edition]), 49.

[75] "Love," in M. Fethullah Gülen, *Criteria, or the Lights of the Way*. London: Truestar Ltd., 1996, 27.

[76] "The Ideal Believer, the Ideal Muslim," Section Three ("The Ideal Human") of *Love and Tolerance*, 163–4. Yunus Emre (ca 1240–1321) was a Sufi poet, a younger contemporary and student of Rumi's poetry and like Rumi, became a leading representative of Sufism in Anatolia on a popular level. Ahmed Yesevi (d. 1166) was also an important Sufi poet, who exerted great influence on developing *tariqa*s within

ment articulates the capacity and the possibility for union between the mystic and the *mysterion*.

Gülen further observes that:

> Love makes one forget his own existence and annihilates his existence in the existence of the beloved. So, it requires the lover to always want his beloved and dedicate himself, without expecting any return, completely to the desires of his beloved. This is, according to my way of thinking, the essence of humanity.[77]

—thus following both the course first laid out by Rabi'a of offering love as the model for the mystical relationship with God and also Rumi's articulation of that process whereby human-human love, that itself yields a condition of being completely subsumed into the beloved, serves as a metaphor for mystical *mahabba* with God's *mysterion*.

Part of that emphasis on *mahabba*, like that in Rabi'a's thought, is both distinctly mystical—i.e., directed beyond the *profanus* to the hidden recesses of (the *mysterion* within) the *sacer*, and, as such, in a sense, theoretical and abstract—and discussed specifically with respect to Muslims:

> Believers love God because He is God, and their love for God is not connected to any earthly or unearthly considerations. They filter and test the gushing springs of love and the waterfalls of their desire for God with the Holy Qur'an and the principles of the most exalted spirit [ie, Muhammad][78]

But Gülen also writes with the goal of redirecting our love focus from the *mysterion* within God *back* to the world created by God, in every corner of which the manifestations of God's Names and Attributes are present. In other words, he articulates the goal of the mystic as not that of gaining access to the *mysterion*, but of gaining access in order

---

the Turkish-speaking world. Both he and Yunus were early writers of poetry in the Turkish vernacular (whereas Rumi wrote mainly in Persian. Some argue that Rumi therefore wrote for a more educated audience. This may not be true, but could be rather a function of his birth and upbringing).

[77] "Love," in *Criteria*, 28.

[78] "Love of God," in Section One ("Love and Mercy"), of *Love and Tolerance*, 50-51.

to *return* from that experience and help improve the world of which we are all part.

On the one hand, this panthenotheistic sensibility—of God's Presence as manifest throughout His creation—and this "fix the world" purpose are shared with important figures within the other Abrahamic mystical traditions, as we have in part noted in the introduction to this narrative. It is particularly emphatic in the work of St. Francis of Assisi within Christian mysticism and of the Ba'al Shem Tov, founder of the Hassidic movement, within Jewish mysticism. On the other hand, Gülen, like they, speaks from within his own tradition; his emphasis turns specifically toward Islam with regard to the issue of understanding and misunderstanding God's presence within and beyond the world in which we live:

> Love is the reason for existence and its essence, and it is the strongest tie that binds creatures together. Everything in the universe is the handiwork of God. Thus, if you do not approach humanity, a creation of God, with love, then you will have hurt those who love God and those whom God loves... ...[O]ur approach to creation and other human beings should be based on loving them for the sake of their Creator. If Muslims talk about weapons, armories, killing and the butchering of others and if by doing so they put vast distances between people, then this means that in fact we have been far removed from our essence.[79]

This perspective—of loving the creation because of its Creator—is articulated again and again by Gülen, citing love as the connecting thread between God and the entire world and not only between God and human beings. It is important to note, however, that Gülen's understanding of God's presence in the world is extremely subtle: he follows an orthodox Sufi understanding of the universe as comprised of the manifestations of Divine Names—thus at once acknowledging the paradox of Divine Names noted by Ibn al-'Arabi; stepping away

---

[79] "Making the Atmosphere of Tolerance Permanent," in Section Two ("Forgiveness, Tolerance and Dialogue") of *Love and Tolerance*, 96. One could spend many pages on Gülen's anti-violence and anti-terrorism, but these stances of his would seem almost too obvious, given his discussions of love, compassion and tolerance, to require extended reference.

from Ibn al-ʿArabi's more direct panhenotheism; and sharing a sense of the paradox of God's Names consonant with yet not identical with God's Essence with mystics in the other (particularly the Jewish) mystical traditions.

Put simply, Gülen views creation as the manifestation of the Names and Attributes of the Creator—*tajalli al-Asma*—rather than as simply seeing the creation as a part of the Creator or seeing both the Creator and the creation as one (*wahdat al-wujud*). This is the sort of distinction that may be seen in the writings of Spinoza toward the beginning of modern Western thought when he distinguishes between God as *Natura naturans* ("nature naturing") and *Natura naturata* ("Nature natured")—but Spinoza removes the concept of an engaged and involved, *personified* God from his formulation, whereas for Gülen the engaged involvement of God in human reality is essential: it provides the ultimate context for love within the human domain.

We are further reminded in a number of passages from Gülen's essays that love is a theme among other figures whom he distinctly recognizes as important and as intellectually and spiritually influential—such as his older Turkish contemporary, Bediüzzaman Said Nursi. Thus:

> God created the universe as a manifestation of His love for His creatures, in particular humanity, and Islam became the fabric woven out of this love. In the words of Bediüzzaman, love is the essence of creation.[80]

In the same passage, Gülen further argues that "'[d]isliking on the way of God' applies only to feelings, thought and attributes. Thus, we should dislike such things as immorality, unbelief, and polytheism, not the people who engage in such activities."[81] Thus even in recognizing the human reality of an incapacity for loving everyone, and in particular of negative feelings toward those whose actions are odious, he emphasizes distinguishing the action from the actor—who is implicitly misguided, not odious. If God is with us and within us all the time,

---

[80] "Islam—A Religion of Tolerance," in Section Two ("Forgiveness, Tolerance and Dialogue") of *Love and Tolerance*, 114.

[81] Ibid, 114.

then to dislike someone may be construed as disliking that manifestation of God reflected in that person.

Moreover, under Gülen's pen the emphasis on love also directs itself beyond abstract theory, yielding guidance for *actions* that *serve* others, as we shall consider in more detail in the following chapter. Foundational expressions of this idea may be found throughout his work. Thus, for instance, in *Love and Tolerance*, in the first essay (entitled "Love"), he argues that

> [a]ltruism is an exalted human feeling, and its course is love. Whoever has the greatest share in this love is the greatest hero of humanity, these people have been able to uproot any feelings of hatred and rancor in themselves. Such heroes of love continue to live even after their death...[82]

Love as a behavioral goal quite naturally leads to and intersects compassion. The one is cognate with the other, for to feel love for others should engender a sense of oneness that bespeaks both being conjoined in their happiness and sharing their feelings, both those that are exhilarating and those that induce suffering.[83] In his essay, "Compassion," in *Towards the Lost Paradise*, Gülen not surprisingly emphasizes the importance of this feeling:

> Compassion is the beginning of being; without it everything is chaos. Everything has come into existence through compassion and by compassion it continues to exist in harmony... Everything speaks of compassion and promises compassion. Because of this, the universe can be considered a symphony of compassion.[84]

But it is not simply that the universe, as a universe of order, is a universe wherein we show compassion to fellow humans, but, resonating from within the tradition of Rumi's all-inclusive emphases, Gülen continues in the same essay to assert:

---

82 "Love," in Section One ("Love and Mercy") of *Love and Tolerance*, 35.

[83] The word "compassion," in fact, derives from the Latin root, "*passio*," meaning "enduring, suffering" and the prefix "*com-*" which means "with" (derived from "*cum*") and, as a prefix, functions as an intensifier.

[84] *Towards the Lost Paradise*. Izmir: Kaynak, 1998, 40.

Man has a responsibility to show compassion to all living beings as a requirement of being human...[85]

Indeed, he goes on to remind us, based on a hadith, that

[w]e hear from the Prophet of Truth that a prostitute went to Paradise because, out of compassion, she gave water to a poor dog dying of thirst, whilst another woman was condemned to the torments of Hell because she left a cat to die of hunger.[86]

Thus his sense of human responsibility for all of creation could not be more emphatic.

His assertion that feeling compassion and allowing such feeling to lead to compassionate actions must be a broadly based process is clear when he writes:

There is no limit to doing others good. One who has dedicated himself to the good of humanity, can be so altruistic as to sacrifice even his life for others. However, such altruism can be a great virtue only so long as it originates in sincerity and purity of intention and the 'others' are not defined by racial preferences.[87]

Moreover, the tone for altruistic behavior could not be more unequivocal: that it originates out of sincerity; and thus that the level of any sort of ulterior motive for such behavior is, as it were, *lower* than zero (it is both altruistic and *sincerely* altruistic)—and the direction of such behavior is toward all of humanity: "others" means potentially anyone and everyone, not only those defined by some ethnic, religious or other sub-category of our species.

Compassion for others leads to what Gülen calls "tolerance." Early on, in a selection from his teachings and preachings published in 1996, he commented:

---

[85] Ibid, 40.

[86] Ibid, 41.

[87] "Humanity," in *Criteria*, 12.

> Be so tolerant that your bosom becomes wide like the ocean. Become
> inspired with faith and love of human beings. Let there be no
> troubled souls to whom you do not offer a hand.[88]

We may recognize in these words a resonance with words that
we have noted in the works of Ibn al-'Arabi and which were then
articulated a number of different places in Rumi's writings: that of a
universal embrace of humanity, as opposed to an approach to human
relations that is sectarian in nature.

As with love and compassion, Gülen returns again and again to the
theme of tolerance:

> Judge your worth in the sight of your Creator by the space you have
> allotted to Him in your heart; and your worth in the eyes of peo-
> ple by the worth of your treatment of them...[89]

And again:

> ... We should have such tolerance that we are able to close our
> eyes to the faults of others, to have respect for different ideas, and
> to forgive everything that is forgivable. In fact, even when faced
> with violations of our inalienable rights, we should remain respect-
> ful to human values and try to establish justice...[90]

And yet again elsewhere—repeating the last sentence, with its
emphasis on respecting human values even vis-a-vis those who per-
form acts that violate those values, and on never ceasing to ally one's self
with justice:

> Our tolerance should be so broad that we can close our eyes to oth-
> ers' faults, show respect for different ideas, and forgive everything
> that is forgivable. Even when our inalienable rights are violated, we
> should respect human values and try to establish justice...[91]

---

[88] "Tolerance," in *Criteria*, 19.

[89] Ibid, 20-21.

[90] "Tolerance", in Section Two ("Forgiveness, Tolerance and Dialogue") of *Love and Tolerance*, 78.

[91] "The Necessity of Interfaith Dialogue," in *Essays—Perspectives—Opinions*, 51.

His ultimate source for such a statement he finds in the Qur'an itself, from which he quotes:

> *If you behave tolerantly, overlook, and forgive (their faults)... (At-Tag-habun* 64:14)[92]

We might note two issues with regard to this universalist perspective. The first is the use of the word "tolerant/tolerance." In general, that word, in English, suggests an unequal nuance: of one party speaking from a higher level regarding a second party, as opposed to referring to an even surface in which equals embrace equals. But in the context in which Gülen uses the term, first of all its Turkish equivalent (and after all, Gülen writes in Turkish), offers a more positive nuance, so that we are in fact dealing with a level-field intention, more equivalent to embrace. He is referring to the full acceptance—and love—of diversely-configured humanity. This full-hearted embrace that his contexts make clear is what he finds in the Qur'an as a guide and what he follows as the path forged by many scholars, such as Ibn al-'Arabi and Rumi, following the Prophet. And thus, second of all, he intends the term to be understood in *opposition* to the term "intolerant," so that it does not merely stand on its own as a concept but is specifically intended to be the anti-concept to intolerance.

That Gülen's intentions through the use of this word are broad and even-looking rather than narrow and downward-looking—and intended to be understood in opposition to those who are not only intolerant but who speak loudly and act forcefully, even violently, on behalf of non-tolerance—is clear from his words spoken at a Ramadan dinner held in the Hilton Hotel in Washington, DC on January 27, 1997. At that World Peace Ramadan Dinner he observed:

> Despite advances in the atmosphere of social tolerance, a marginal group still spoils social peace by screaming and shouting to make it appear that they are strong... traps will be set for tolerance. They're going to try to destroy the bridges...[but] we are going to walk

---

[92] "Tolerance," in Section Two ("Forgiveness, Tolerance and Dialogue") of *Love and Tolerance*, 80.

toward tomorrow by embracing everything with love and compassion and by loving each other.[93]

If there is something about which he is intolerant, it is intolerance and those who advocate it. But his conviction is that those who believe in universal love, compassion and tolerance—mutual embrace—will ultimately win out.

And not surprisingly, he is more precise and explicit about the unequivocally positive and even-grounded intention of the term in his essay, "Tolerance," found in the compendium that, entitled *Love and Tolerance*, is arguably the consummate summary of his thinking on the subject of described and prescribed human behavior. There he explicitly equates tolerance with an array of terms for which only the most positive of interpretations is possible:

> Tolerance, a term which we sometimes use in place of the words respect, mercy, generosity, or forbearance, is the most essential element of moral systems; it is a very important source of spiritual discipline and a celestial virtue of perfected people.[94]

Indeed, (to repeat), Gülen demands from those who follow him that they be tolerant of all of humanity—to have hearts "wide like the ocean" and to seek to become more perfect human beings (for "[t]he most perfect among human beings are those who are at ease and intimate in the company of other human beings [ie, *all* human beings]").[95] Conversely,

> Those who do not embrace all of humankind with tolerance and forgiveness have lost their worthiness to receive forgiveness and pardon... Those who curse will be cursed and those who beat will be beaten. If true Muslims observe such Qur'anic principles as the fol-

---

[93] This was quoted in an article by the journalist Sakir Suter in *Aksam* daily, on January 29, 1997, and reproduced in Ali Unal & Alphonse Williams, eds., *Fethullah Gülen, Advocate of Dialogue*. (Fairfax, VA: The Fountain, 2000), 213.

[94] The essay appears in Section Two ("Forgiveness, Tolerance and Dialogue"), 78. The same two sentences appear in "The Necessity of Interfaith Dialogue, in *Essays— Perspectives—Opinions*, 52, with the slight difference that he replaces the word "people" with the phrase "men and women" at the end of the second sentence.

[95] "Humility," in *Criteria*, 23.

lowing and were to go on their way and tolerate curses deep in their breasts, then others would appear in order to implement the justice of Destiny on those who cursed us.[96]

He thus defines "Muslim" as someone who conforms to his description of being tolerant. His view of Islam, simply put, is of a faith that exemplifies the principles which he embeds in the word "tolerance."

He is thus clear that breadth of perspective does not mean abandoning one's own way of being, but of recognizing the features of that way that are also found in others' ways of being, the recognizing of which improves the life of all and thus improves the world:

> Being tolerant does not mean foregoing the traditions that come from our religion, or our nation, or our history; tolerance is something that has always existed. The Ottomans were faithful both to their religion and to other values and, at the same time, they were a great nation that could get along with other world states... In the name of dialogue we can unite on common ground and shake hands with all. This is because the things that God gives most value to are human beings, love, and compassion.[97]

Again and again Gülen emphasizes the importance of tolerance, the desideratum of loving all of humanity, and the need to actively engage those in other faith traditions through dialogue. This path is a "road [that] is open to everybody. Nonetheless it is essential that the traveler be sincere and determined."[98] Thus on the one hand, false embrace—tolerance which is downward-looking—closes the road; and on the other hand, since it is not always an easy road—learning to truly love those whose perspective, spiritual and otherwise, is different from one's own may be challenging. Gaining the trust of other dialogicians may be slow, but one must not be easily turned back.

The inspiration for both taking that road and recognizing it as open to everyone and anyone Gülen finds in the way of being in the world exemplified by Prophet Muhammad himself:

---

[96] "Tolerance," in Section Two ("Forgiveness, Tolerance and Dialogue,") of *Love and Tolerance*, 80.

[97] "Tolerance in the Life of the Individual and Society," in Ibid, 90-91.

[98] "Love of God," in Section One ("Love and Mercy") of *Love and Tolerance*, 50.

More than anything else, with the training he received from his Lord, the Pride of Humankind [i.e., Muhammad] gave value to every human being, regardless of whether that person was a Muslim, Christian or Jew.[99]

The inspiration for taking the road is the array of hadiths that report on the Prophet—that

> When he was dying and about to pass over to the next world, he said: *I place in your trust the People of the Book, the Christians and Jews.* [Abu Dawud, Imarah, 33; Muttaqi al-Hindi, Kanz al-Ummal, 4, 362][100]

The inspiration for taking the road is the array of hadiths that report on the first four caliphs—the *rashidun*, the "rightly-guided" successors of the Prophet as leaders of the Muslim community, who strove most strenuously to emulate the Prophet in their thoughts, words and actions:

> When Umar had been stabbed and was in the throes of death, he warned: *I place the People of the Book among us in your trust. Fear God regarding them and treat them justly.* [Yahya ibn Adam, Kitab al-Haraj, 54.][101]

The inspiration for taking the road and maintaining one's pace along it derives from historical figures like Salahaddin, quoted by Gülen as saying to Richard the Lion-Hearted: "… I fully believe that the coming years will be years of tolerance and love."[102]

The inspiration for both taking the road and recognizing its open breadth is Rumi and others inspired by Rumi, such as the Turkish poet, Yunus Emre (ca 1238–1320):

> From this word [tolerance] we understand embracing people regardless of differences of opinion, world-view, ideology, ethnicity, or

[99] "Tolerance in the Life of the Individual and Society," in Section Two ("Forgiveness, Tolerance and Dialogue,") of *Love and Tolerance*, 91.

[100] "Without Hands Against Those Who Strike You, Without Speech Against Those Who Curse You", in Ibid, 107.

[101] Ibid, 108.

[102] Ibid, 108.

belief....From another approach, it means, in the words of the famous Turkish poet Yunus, loving the created simply because of the Creator.[103]

Moreover,

> If we can spread the Islamic understanding of such heroes of love as Niyazi-i Misri, Yunus Emre, and Rumi globally, if we can extend their messages of love, dialogue, and tolerance to those who thirst for this message, then everyone will run toward the embrace of love, peace, and tolerance we represent.[104]

So, too, the references made to dialogue and mutual respect specifically among the Abrahamic faiths are extensive in Gülen's writing. Any number of passages might be singled out to be of particular note in this regard. They are found most obviously in an array of different essays in the volume, *Love and Tolerance*. Thus he writes:

> When God sent Moses and Aaron to a man who claimed to possess divinity, as the Pharaoh had done, He commanded them to behave tolerantly and to speak softly. (See Sura *Ta-Ha* 20:44):[105]

This passage is of double interest. It underscores the importance to Muhammad and the Qur'an of prior prophets—those embraced by Jews and Christians—that is well recognized by Gülen. And by extension, if Moses is being enjoined to be tolerant—to engage in respectful dialogue—with a pagan ruler who thinks of himself as God, how much the more so must we (Muslims) be tolerant of and engage in respectful dialogue with Jews and Christians whose differences of belief

---

[103] "Making the Atmosphere of Tolerance Permanent," in Ibid, *Love and Tolerance*, 95. As noted above (fn # 76), Yunus Emre was a Sufi poet, a younger contemporary of Rumi and like Rumi, became a leading representative of Sufism in Anatolia on a popular level.

[104] "Islam—A Religion of Tolerance", in Section Two ("Forgiveness, Tolerance and Dialogue") of *Love and Tolerance*, 115. Niyazi-i Misri was a Sufi poet from the Khalwati *tariqa*, and lived 1618-94. Gülen repeats virtually this same sentence in his essay, "Real Muslims Cannot Be Terrorists," in Section Five of the same volume, 289, but excluding Niyazi-i Misri from mention.

[105] "Tolerance and Dialogue in the Qur'an and the Sunna" in Section Two ("Forgiveness, Tolerance and Dialogue") of *Love and Tolerance*, 128. This Sura's name is exceptional in that it is simply the two letters—"*ta*" and "*ha*"—that make up the first verse.

from our own are so much less profound than those between the Pha-
raoh and Moses?

Directly addressing the issue of dialogue with Jews and Christians, Gülen continues in the same essay:

> In addition to being commanded to take tolerance and to use dia-
> logue as his basis while performing his duties, the Prophet was
> directed to those aspects in which he had things in common with
> the People of the Book (Jews and Christians): *Say, "O People of the
> book! Come to common terms as between us and you: that we worship
> none but God; that we attribute no partners with Him; that we take
> not some from among ourselves for Lords other than God."* (Al Imran
> ["The Family of Imran"] 3:64)[106]

Further,

> [An] aspect of establishing and maintaining dialogue is the neces-
> sity of increasing the interests we have in common with other peo-
> ple. In fact, even if the people we talk with are Jews and Christians,
> this approach still should be adopted and issues that separate us
> should be avoided altogether... ...Our common point is belief in
> God...[107]

Moreover,

> ..[E]xcept in certain special cases, the Qur'an and the Sunna always
> advocate tolerance. The shielding canopy of this tolerance extends
> not only to the People of the Book, but, in a sense, to all people.[108]

The shared ideas and convictions that invite Abrahamic dialogue
are a frequent reference point for him, as, for example:

> There are many common points for dialog among devout Muslims,
> Christians, and Jews. As pointed out by Michael Wyschogrod, an
> American pioneer of philosophy, there are just as many theoretical

---

[106] Ibid, 128–29.

[107] "Dialogue in the Muhammadan Spirit and Meaning," in Section Two ("Forgiveness,
Tolerance and Dialogue") of *Love and Tolerance*, 133.

[108] Ibid, 138.

or creedal reasons for Muslims and Jews drawing closer to one another as there are for Jews and Christian coming together.[109]

—as are both his view of the *imperative* of dialogue and his belief in its wide-ranging potential inclusiveness:

> The goal of dialog among world religions is not simply to destroy scientific materialism and the destructive materialistic worldview; rather, the very nature of religion demands this dialog. Judaism, Christianity, and Islam, and even Hinduism and other world religions accept the same source for themselves, and including Buddhism, pursue the same goal.[110]

Thus his vision of dialogue extends beyond the Abrahamic traditions. While Gülen repeats in several places the historical-conceptual reason for the logic and importance of mutual tolerance and of dialogue among the Abrahamic traditions, he also repeats the imperative that dialogue take place—not only among practitioners of these three faiths but with those outside them—in which conviction he distinctly echoes what was, as we have seen, articulated by Ibn al-'Arabi and expanded as an idea by Rumi:

> Islam, Christianity and Judaism all stem from the same root; all have essentially the same basic beliefs, and are nourished from the same source. Although they have lived as rival religions for centuries, the common points between them and their shared responsibility to build a happy world for all of the creatures of God make interfaith dialogue among them necessary. This dialogue has now expanded to include the religions of Asia and other areas. The results have been positive.[111]

Or more simply and more emphatically put:

---

[109] "The Necessity of Interfaith Dialogue," in *Essays—Perspectives—Opinions*, 35. Wyschogrod is a prominent contemporary Jewish thinker for whose thought Gülen expresses a strong affinity.

[110] Ibid, 34.

[111] "At the Threshold of a New Millennium," in Section Seven ("Global Perspectives") of *Love and Tolerance*, 362.

> There are as many roads to God as there are creatures. God leads
> those who struggle for His sake to salvation on one or more of
> these roads...[112]

More to the point, it is because of God's omnipresence within creation and all of its creatures and the endless ways in which the manifestations of God may be refracted through them that, in partaking of
that one, endlessly refractable God, those creatures are and do what
they are and do. Recognizing the refracted manifestations of God within each other should yield to mutual love and respect, compassion and
dialogue:

> ... As an individual of the universal chorus, almost every creature
> acts and behaves in its own style, according to the magical tune it
> has received from God, in a melody of love. However, this exchange
> of love from existence to humanity and from one creature to anoth-
> er takes place beyond their will, because the Divine Will complete-
> ly dominates them.[113]

This is not to say that dialogue can or should be presented as
always and necessarily a simple matter. But just as Gülen differs from
Rumi in the specific ways in which he addresses the subject of dialogue
as a desideratum and a necessity—for the world of the late twentieth
and early twenty-first centuries in which Gülen lives is a vaster one, in
which communication across that vastness is virtually instantaneous,
as compared with the thirteenth-century world through which Rumi
moved—so Gülen recognizes the complications that attend interdenominational dialogue today.

As much as Rumi's world was the world that culminated more than
two centuries of Crusader conflict between Christians and Muslims
(in which it is fair to say that the Christians conducted themselves more
often with more cruelty and disrespect of other humans than did the

---

[112] "Lesser and Greater Jihad," in Section Five ("Jihad—Terrorism and Human Rights")
of *Love and Tolerance*, 279.

[113] "Humanism and Love of Humanity," in Section One ("Love and Mercy") of *Love
and Tolerance*, 43.

Muslims),[114] Gülen's world is a world much of which still remembers those events but in which, moreover, more unhappy events have taken place in the course of the many intervening centuries.

Gülen addresses the inevitable complications that attend a process that has as a natural starting point the possibility of suspicion, doubt and a painful history. He notes that:

> ... [In the Qur'an] it is stated: *God forbids you not, with regard to those who fight you not for (your) Faith nor drive you out of your homes, from dealing kindly and justly with them; for God loves those who are just.* (60:8)[115]

> According to some, several verses harshly criticize the People of the Book. In reality, such criticism is directed against wrong behavior, incorrect thought, resistance to truth, the creation of hostility, and undesirable characteristics. The Bible contains even stronger criticisms of the same attributes. However, immediately after these apparently sharp criticisms and threats, very gentle words are used to awaken hearts to the truth and to plant hope. In addition, the Qur'an's criticism and warning about some attitudes and behavior found among Jews, Christians, and polytheists also were directed toward Muslims who still indulge in them.[116]

Thus "we" includes all reasonable people; "them" includes all unreasonable people, i.e., fanatics, terrorists, and the like. If there is a line that is difficult to cross it is that between *these* two categories of humans and not those between different religious or ethnic or national categories.

Certain groups of Muslims may be slow to arrive at a desire for dialogue, perhaps slower than their Christian counterparts, but some Christians may also doubt the sincerity of Muslim expressions of the desire for genuine dialogue:

> ...the Church's call for dialog meets with considerable suspicion. [Conversely], [p]erceiving Islam as a party ideology in some Muslim

---

[114] See the ebullient account of this by one of the leaders of the first Crusade, Godfrey of Bouillon, of the taking of Jerusalem and the rivers of blood of Jews and Muslims reaching up to the haunches of his horse.

[115] Sura 60 is called *al-Mumtahinah* ("The Test" or "She Who Is to Be Examined").

[116] "The Necessity of Interfaith Dialogue," in *Essays—Perspectives—Opinions*. 47.

countries, including Turkey [has led] secularists and others... to look
upon all Muslims and Islamic societies as suspect.[117]

Or the process may be undercut because "Christendom's historical portrayal of Islam also has weakened Muslims' courage with respect
to interfaith dialog."[118] But nonetheless,

> Interfaith dialog is a must today, and the first step in establishing it is
> forgetting the past, ignoring polemical arguments, and giving prece-
> dence to common points, which far outnumber polemical ones.[119]

For dialogue is an inherent part of Islam:

> The Qur'an calls the People of the Book: Say, "*O People of the Book!*
> *Come to common terms as between us and you: that we worship none*
> *but God...*" (3:64) ...In case this call was rejected, Muslims were to
> respond: *Your religion is for you; my religion is for me.* (109:6)[120]

Gülen finds the basis, justification and importance of dialogue, as
he finds the basis, justification and importance of embracing the broadest range of participants in one's engagement in a sweep of Muslim
texts that carry from the Qur'an and the hadith forward through the
Sufi tradition as it continues into the twentieth century in the person
of Bediüzzaman Said Nursi, Gülen's much-admired predecessor. He
associates dialogue and inclusiveness not only with love, compassion
and tolerance but with true freedom and human salvation:

> ...this broad path of salvation, and this law of freedom [is part of
> Islam in its broadest scope]... Bediüzzaman Said Nursi explains this
> broadest scope of Islam from a contemplative observation he had
> in the Beyazıt Mosque in Istanbul:
>
> Once I thought about the pronoun "we" in the verse: *You alone do we*
> *worship, and You alone we ask for help* (1:5),[121] and my heart sought
> the reason why "we" was used in place of "I." Suddenly I discov-

---

[117] Ibid, 36–7.

[118] Ibid, 37.

[119] Ibid. 38.

[120] Ibid, 43. Sura 109 is called *al-Kafirun* ("The Disbelievers").

[121] The opening chapter of the Qur'an is called simply *al-Fatihah*—"The Opening"—and
serves as a statement of praise to God and a request for spiritual guidance from Him.

ered the virtue and secret of congregational prayer from that pronoun "we."

I saw that by doing my prayer with the congregation at the Beyazit Mosque, every individual in the congregation became a kind of intercessor for me...

... I felt I was standing in prayer in front of the blessed Ka'ba... I saw that the congregation I was in was separated into three circles.

The first circle was a large congregation of believing Muslims and those who believe in God's existence and unity. In the second circle, I saw [that] all creatures were performing the greatest prayer and invocation of God. Every class or species was busy with its own unique invocation and litanies to God and I was among the congregation. In the third circle I saw an amazing realm that was outwardly small, but in reality, large from the perspective of the duty it performed and its quality. From the atoms of my body to the outer senses, there was a congregation busy with servitude and gratitude.

In short, the pronoun "we" in the expression "we worship" pointed to these three congregations.[122]

Where Gülen might be seen to differ from Nursi is in the word "separate." In a very obvious way each individual, every mosque, each denominational congregation within and beyond the Muslim world, humanity as opposed to other creatures large and small, and animal species rather than plants or rocks—all are separate from each other. But Gülen's writings suggest his sense that part of the point of a doctrine of love, compassion, tolerance and also, among humans, of dialogue, is that we are interwoven threads in an unimaginably large fabric. The lines of separation are simultaneously distinct and completely blurred—and the condition of blurring does not eliminate our distinctnesses as beings and as groups of beings any more than our distinctness should allow us to ignore our interwovenness.

But Nursi is a reference point not only for shaping a sense of interdenominational inclusiveness, as Rumi so emphatically is, but also for

---

[122] "The Necessity of Interfaith Dialogue," in *Essays—Perspectives—Opinions,* 38-39.

how, practically, to begin the process of dialogue by seeking points of commonality rather than dwelling on divisive issues at the outset:

> Bediuzzaman drew attention to solutions and the future. Saying that "controversial subjects shouldn't be discussed with Christian spiritual leaders," he opened dialogues with members of other religions. Like Jalal al-Din al-Rumi, who said "One of my feet is in the center and the other is in seventy-two realms (people of all nations) like a compass," he drew a broad circle that encompasses all mono-theists.[123]

How *does* one begin? Gülen continues, in the same essay:

> At the very outset, using a very soft and slightly oblique style, the Qur'an calls people to accept the former Prophets and their Books. Having such a condition at the very beginning of the Qur'an [2:3–4] seems very important to me when it comes to starting a dialog with the followers of other religions. In another verse God commands: *And discuss you not with the People of the Book, except with means better (than mere disputation)* (29:46) This verse describes what method, approach, and manner should be used. Bediuzzaman's view of the form and style of debate are extremely significant: "Anyone who is happy about defeating an opponent in debate is without mercy." He explains further: "You gain nothing by such a defeat. If you were defeated and the other was victorious, you would have corrected one of your mistakes." Debate should not be for the sake of our ego, but to enable the truth to come out.[124]

He confirms that the point and purpose of dialogue is not conversionary; it is not to win an argument regarding whose understanding of God is superior. It is to learn to understand and eventually, through that understanding, to come to love the other for the common humanity—and for the implanted divinity—found in all of us. This is distinctly "tolerance" not as a downward-looking process but as an even-looking—and therefore forward-looking, idealistic—process.

In his essay, "Love for Humankind" Gülen may be said to summarize in the broadest possible terms what this is about, connecting love for humanity with a still more-encompassing love of the planet in all

---

[123] "M. Fethullah Gülen on Education," in *Essays—Perspectives—Opinions*, 86.
[124] "The Necessity of Interfaith Dialogue," in *Essays—Perspectives—Opinions*, 46-7.

of its components, and reminding the reader of the place of Rumi as a key foundation stone in the edifice of such a sensibility. As such, Gülen is not simply universalizing by losing contact with his Muslim heritage, but explaining Islam as a spiritual perspective that inherently recognizes the principle of universalism and pointing to Rumi as a particularly adept exponent of that principle:

> Our interest in our environment and our love for humankind—that is, our ability to embrace creation—depends on knowing and understanding our own essence, our ability to discover ourselves, and to feel a connection with our Creator. In parallel with the ability to discover and feel our inner depths and hidden potential within our essence, we will also be able to appreciate that others also possess the same potential... In reality, the level of our understanding and appreciation of one another depends on how well we recognize the qualities and riches that each person possesses. We can summarize this concept with a thought based on a saying of the Prophet, peace and blessings be unto him, "A believer is the mirror of another believer." We can enlarge on this saying as "a human is a mirror of another human."... [W]e will also understand how to relate these riches to their true Owner, and thus we will accept that anything in this universe that is beautiful, affectionate, or loving belongs to Him. A soul that can sense this depth says, as did Rumi presenting us tales from the language of the heart: "Come, come and join us, as we are the people of love devoted to God! Come, come through the door of love and join us and sit with us. Come, let us speak one to another through our hearts. Let us speak secretly, without ears and eyes. Let us laugh together without lips or sound, let us laugh like the roses. Like thought, let us see each other without any words or sounds. Since all are the same, let us call each other from our hearts, we won't use our lips or tongue. As our hands are clasped together, let us talk about it."... Islamic thought sees each one of us as a different manifestation of a unique ore, as different aspects of one reality. ...[125]

This breadth of focus—on all of humankind and also on the natural environment, in which latter focus and concern Gülen carries a Rumi-inspired view of God's Presence with the manifestations of His Names throughout His creation more explicitly outward than does his

---

[125] "Love for Humankind," in Section One ("Love and Mercy") of *Love and Tolerance*, 40-41.

thirteenth-century co-religionist—derives directly from the Qur'an itself, and the passage in which humanity is said to be charged with a vice-regency responsibility for the world which God created. Gülen asserts:

> Humanity's vicegerency for the Creator takes place in an unusually broad sphere that encompasses acts ranging from believing Him and worshipping Him to understanding the mysteries within things and the cause of natural phenomena, and therefore being able to inter-fere in nature. Throughout their lives, genuine human beings first arrange their feelings and thoughts, regulating their individual and social life through various forms of worship, balancing familial and social relationship by their actions ...This is the true nature of a vice-regent and at the same time this is where the meaning of what it is to be a servant and lover of God can be found.[126]

These last few lines articulate the principle that shepherding each other and the world around us are ultimately modes of serving and loving God—they are concomitants of worshipping within the mosque. He links the act of worship in the familiar, traditional mode—of recit-ing a prescribed series of prayers five times daily together with what-ever occasional verbal expressions of praise or thanksgiving one might direct toward God in the course of a day[127]—with actions that both explore and preserve the natural world. Thus he directs his thoughts also—in a way that would no doubt have seemed somewhat foreign to Rumi and other medieval Sufi thinkers, but certainly not to a thinker like Bediüzzaman Said Nursi—toward science and its potential role not only in improving the human condition in the here and now but in connecting ourselves more fully to God:

---

[126] "Humanity and Its Responsibilities," in Section Three (The Ideal Human") of *Love and Tolerance*, 208. For a more detailed discussion of Gülen's engagement of the concept of human vice-regency as it applies specifically to environmental concerns, see Ori Z Soltes, "Fethullah Gülen and Eco-Justice: From Genesis 1:28 and Qur'an 2:30 to Platonic *ergon* and Aristotelian *harmonia*," in Kim, Heon and John Raines (eds), *Making Peace In and With the World: The Role of the Gülen Movement in Eco-Justice*, (Newcastle UK: Cambridge Scholars Publishing), 2012.

[127] While Islam prescribes formal prayer—*salat*—five times daily (at dawn, noon, mid-afternoon, evening, and night), informal prayer, called *du'a*, is welcome at any time under any circumstances.

> Worship... is the clearest expression of the relationship amongst humans, the universe and God. [Worshippers] ...will walk in the greatest spiritual ecstasy, overstepping the boundaries of existence and reaching Eden.[128]

Part of what is distinctive about Gülen's thinking and variously distinguishes him from all the predecessors from whose thought he draws inspiration is the direction to which he carries the notions expressed in these last few passages. He expands the articulation of concern for the environment and of perceiving a connectedness not only among humans but between humans and the natural environment, the world at large and God. His Sufi sensibilities—that find God's Presence everywhere and therefore seek the *mysterion* not only by withdrawing into one's innermost being in order to step beyond one's self and into God's hiddenmost being—not only recognize sibling searches within other traditions. They recognize that, for Islam to be part of the forefront of that search, it may not—it must not—turn its back on the ongoing developments within scientific thinking and research.

Of course it would not have occurred to Rumi to promote the study of natural sciences—we have seen that he places them in a position ambiguously equal to or below, but certainly not above the mystical process. The world in which he lived was one in which Islam was in any case already at the forefront of new developments along those lines. His only concern would have been that people not get so caught up in the process of human accomplishment with regard to the natural world that they forget the ultimate source of both that world and humanity.

By contrast, Nursi was thinking and writing during an era when the intellectual greatness and grandeur that had once defined the Ottoman and other Muslim powers had waned dramatically—followed by an era, within Turkey, of determined turning against Muslim sensibilities toward secularism. So his concern was to demonstrate to the secular Turkish authorities and more so, to the Turkish nation, that it ought

---

[128] "Humanity and Its Responsibilities," in Section Three (The Ideal Human") of *Love and Tolerance*, 208-9.

not become deracinated and alienated from its own Muslim roots. For him it became a desideratum to demonstrate specific ways in which scientific thinking was to be found and scientific accomplishments anticipated in the basic Muslim texts of the Qur'an and hadith.

Gülen's place in Turkey and in the Muslim and general worlds follows rather naturally in the footsteps taken by Nursi, but articulated in his own very emphatic manner. On the one hand, the foundational element within the thinking of both is faith. In his essay, "Faith: A Particular Perspective," he quotes extensively from Nursi, as for example:

> ...Indeed, "faith is both light and power. Those who attain true faith can challenge the universe and, in proportion to their faith's strength, be relieved of the pressures of events." This is because "faith leads to testifying to God's uniqueness, this testimony leads to submission, submission leads to putting oneself in God's hands, and this last leads to happiness here and in the hereafter."[129]

On the other hand, Gülen's extensive discussion of science, while it may be seen to have a certain degree of root matter in Nursi's desire to show how scientific discovery accords with and fulfills Qur'anic dicta, clearly charts its own path. Gülen emphasizes the importance of science both in general and for Islam—precisely so that, in step with the contemporary world, Islam will be better positioned to articulate the principles of love, compassion, tolerance and dialogue to the world. Thus on the one hand:

> We can only imagine a new, better world based on knowledge or science if we look at the concept of science through the prism of metaphysics. Muslims have not yet developed a concept of science in its true meaning, namely, one derived from the Qur'an and Islamic traditions primarily shaped by the Qur'an and hadiths.[130]

Thus one can embrace scientific universals without rejecting Islamic (or other) particulars—in which view Gülen echoes but refines Nursi's

---

[129] "Faith: A Particular Perspective," in Section Four ("Sufism and Metaphysics") of *Love and Tolerance*, 138. He is quoting from Nursi's *The Words*: "Twenty-third Word."

[130] "Horizons of the Soul: Metaphysical Thought," in Section Four ("Sufism and Metaphysics"), of *Love and Tolerance*, 244.

view. But on the other hand he simply and straightforwardly sees science as important for us as human beings, Muslim or otherwise, who would be part of the process of improving the world around us and thus acting as junior partners with the God who created it and us and imbued us with the capacity to learn in ways other species cannot, imposing upon us the condition of vice-regency over and responsibility for the earth. We must be constantly thinking about the natural world around us, never ceasing to ask ourselves how to fulfill this responsibility, as surely as we must constantly have God before our inner eye as a reminder of that responsibility.

Thus,

> [r]ight decisions depend on having a sound mind and on sound thinking. What illuminates and develops mind is science and knowledge. For this reason, a mind deprived of science and knowledge cannot reach right decisions and is always exposed to deception and subject to being misled.[131]

Moreover,

> ... just as the past was not without science, so too, the future cannot be without it; everything in the end is connected with science. A world without some science has nothing to give to man.[132]

We might understand his reference to the past in both general and specifically Islamic terms, since Islam led the sciences forward for centuries. And clearly one of Gülen's concerns is that the Muslim world take up the banner of science with enthusiasm once again, bringing to its cause the spiritual breadth and depth that are the Islamic hallmarks that he champions. Thus passages such as,

> "Instead of being opposed to the products of science and technology, it is necessary to use them so as to bring happiness to man..."[133]

may also be understood as directed mainly at those among his co-religionists who remain wary of the sciences and misconstrue the Proph-

---

[131] "What We Can Expect of Science," in *Criteria*, 31
[132] "Regrets about Science and Technology," in *Towards the Lost Paradise*, 74.
[133] Ibid, 76.

et's own ongoing thirst for knowledge. For that thirst was a component of the wisdom with which Muhammad sought to improve the human condition.

But as when in the discussion of dialogue, Gülen recognizes the historical complications that prevent the process of simply unfolding without bumps on the road, so where science is concerned he notes that

> [t]he general atmosphere and conditions surrounding us promise great happiness so long as science and technology with all their facilities and fruits are devoted to the service of humanity. Nevertheless, so far we have not been able to make proper use of these extensive possibilities. The happiness of humanity has been delayed.[134]

Moreover,

> It is... true that in some of our cities man has been reduced, human feelings have been diminished, certain human virtues together with health and ability to think have been wiped out. But it is an injustice to ascribe all this to science and technology. The fault lies rather with the scientists who avoid their responsibilities.[135]

and

> ...Science and its products will not cease to be harmful to mankind until the men of truth assume the direction of things and events....[136]

The last part of the second of these brief passages is also part of a series of reminders that, indeed, science without a spiritual underpinning can all too easily end up harming and not helping humankind. This Gülen recognizes as the obvious course of events that carried the glories of the Western Industrial Revolutions of the 1760s through the early twentieth century relentlessly forward, toward the disasters that defined the twentieth century from August, 1914 onward—and which legacy is still being felt into the early twenty-first century. He points not only to the obvious horrors of war, but to other byproducts of mismanaging scientific acumen through ignoring both the breadth of

---

[134] Ibid, 74.
[135] Ibid, 75.
[136] Ibid, 76.

human need and the divinely implanted elements within both humans and the world around us. Thus

> Underlying pollution's global threat is the understanding, brought about by scientific unbelief, that nature is an accumulation of things that have no value other than meeting bodily needs. In fact, nature is much more than a heap of materiality or an accumulation of objects: It has a certain sacredness, for it is an arena in which God's Beautiful Names are displayed. ...Nature is an exhibition of beauty and meaning that displays such profound and vast meanings in the form of trees taking root, flowers blossoming, fruit producing taste and aroma, rain, streams flowing, air breathed in and out, and soil acting as a wet-nurse to innumerable creatures...[137]

It is this sense of nature that is expressed in the panhenotheistic exclamations of Ibn al-'Arabi and even more so, of Rumi, whose words are wells from which Gülen drinks deeply—and which he then turns to apply to the issue of science and the responsibility of scientists to recognize nature for what it is and thus to use their knowledge to enhance, rather than to destroy nature.

Ultimately,

> [s]cience means comprehending what things and events tell us, and what the Divine Laws prevailing over the universe reveal to us. It means striving to understand the purpose of the Creator. Man, who has been created in order that he shall rule over all things, needs to observe, read, discern and learn about what is around him.[138]

Thus the role of human vice-regency announced in the Qur'an, and to which role Gülen frequently refers, finds an obvious focal point in properly pursued scientific inquiry. If the scientist's goal is to improve the human condition then he is part of the vice-regency process and science and religion have no quarrel with each other. This is what Albert Einstein, arguably the leading scientist of the twentieth century, observed when he wrote that, whereas science can tell us what is, religion's purpose is to tell us how we should use the knowledge of what is that we

---

[137] "M.Fethullah Gülen on Education," in *Essays—Perspectives—Opinions*, 83.
[138] "Regrets about Science and Technology," in *Towards the Lost Paradise*, 75.

gain from science.[139] Like Einstein, Gülen emphasizes how the two areas of human enterprise must function hand-in-hand for the betterment of the world. He writes:

> Religion and science are, in fact, two faces of a single truth. Religion guides man to the true path leading to happiness. As for science, when understood and used properly, it is like a torch which provides man with a light to follow on that very same path.[140]

Indeed,

> Science and knowledge should seek to uncover the nature of man and the mysteries of creation. Any knowledge, however 'scientific,' is no 'true knowledge' if it does not shed light on the mysteries of human nature and the dark areas of existence.[141]

For ultimately, "[t]he purpose of learning is to make knowledge a guide in life and illuminate the road to human betterment…"[142] If we are not accomplishing that through science then the validity of scientific exploration is significantly undercut.

Moreover, in considering the issue of human betterment, the question of what constitutes "human" inevitably comes up in the discussion of science precisely with the intention of validating it as a partner with spiritual seeking as an element of humanity. Thus Gülen notes that

> …It is difficult to regard as truly human someone who is ignorant and has no desire to learn. It is also questionable whether a learned person who does not renew and reform himself so as to set an example for others is truly human.[143]

In this notion we hear echoes of another thinker important to Gülen: Socrates. For the ancient Athenian father of Western philosophy, as we hear him articulated through the writings of his disciple, Plato, had been wont to observe that "the unexamined life is not worth

---

[139] Albert Einstein, "Science and Religion", in *Out of My Later Years*. New York: Philosophical Library, Chapter 8.

[140] "Religion," in *Criteria*, 7.

[141] "What We Can Expect of Science," in *Criteria*, 32.

[142] Ibid, 32.

[143] Ibid, 31.

living," and that those who don't examine the world and explore and seek to explain it—to ask questions about it and about what is beyond it—are not making full use of their human capacities. Gülen's emphasis on scientific inquiry may be seen, in part, as part of his interweave of threads woven by specific Islamic thinkers like Rumi and Nursi (and others) with those woven by a range of non-Muslim thinkers.

To repeat: the interweave recognizes religion—the interest in a reality beyond our own—as being as essential to the condition of being human as the interest in exploring our own reality is. Thus

> It is by means of religion that a man is elevated in spirit and feelings so high that he makes contact with the metaphysical worlds, from where he is "fed" to full satisfaction with all kinds of beauties, virtues and goodness.
>
> ...A man attains true humanity by means of religion, and is thereby distinguished from animals. For the irreligious, there is no difference between human beings and animals...[144]

Gülen would thus clearly understand the abandonment of religion and therefore of God by various scientists as a root cause for the disasters wrought by means of science and its "advancements" over the past century and more. His view is that the future salvation of humankind requires an emphatic partnership between science and religion.

* * * * *

It is moreover also arguable that, together with the principles of universal love, compassion and tolerance; the insistence on the importance of dialogue; and the advocacy for scientific inquiry from within a religious framework; the most important issue argued over the years by Gülen is that thoughts and words are not enough to make a difference in a world that needs our care if it is to be a happier place for our children and grandchildren. Thus he repeatedly articulates the idea offered in his early published writing, as a complement to the words just quoted:

---

[144] "Religion," in *Criteria*, 10.

> The most distinctive feature of a soul overflowing with faith is to
> love the love expressed in deeds, and to feel enmity for the deeds
> in which enmity is expressed.[145]

Three issues are engaged here. One is that of *hizmet*—service: expressions of love for humanity is best stated in actions—deeds—that serve, that "offer a hand" to any and all "troubled souls" needing it. Interwoven with this is a second issue, that *hizmet* expressed in actions should be universally directed as an expression of faith—for Gülen does not define the faith to which he refers in sectarian terms.

The third issue is that when he uses the term "enmity" it is directed against enmity itself: one should feel hostile to hostility, one should hate hatred, not hate, feel hostility or enmity to people (even those who are hostile or who hate). This is a simple, strong statement which is articulated numerous times by him over the years.

In reiterating the principle that Gülen draws from diverse sources, one might say that through this third issue he has applied the Socratic-Platonic principles that "to know the good is to do the good" and that "to harm someone else ultimately harms the one who has committed the harm far more than it does his victim, since it is the victimizer's immortal soul that is damaged by bad actions" to his own contexts.[146] Gülen's notion that one should not direct hatred or hostility toward others would suggest a sense that such sentiments ultimately damage the one feeling them: that if one fails to galvanize one's energies toward eradicating bad acts because of expending it on the people who commit them, one ultimately fails to improve the human condition and the world at large, which is harmful to everyone and everything, including, of course, one's self.

---

[145] "Tolerance," in *Criteria*, 20.

[146] This is most beautifully expressed, perhaps, in the course of Socrates' speech before the Athenian court that judged and convicted him, the *Apology*. One also gets aspects of the second idea in the *Crito* and the *Protagoras*. Since Socrates wrote nothing down, what we know of this thinking we know mainly from Plato, his prize pupil. Classicists have debated for centuries where the line is properly drawn between where Socrates' thought leaves off and Plato's begins. For our purposes the distinction does not matter, since it is the thought and not the thinker, per se, that is at issue. And these sentiments are repeated in many places in the Platonic corpus.

The Socratic principle that the one who commits harm is hurt more than the one whom he harms may also be seen as reflected in Gülen's argument that every "self" is related to all "selves" and therefore that every action that benefits someone else may be seen to benefit the one who acts as much as it benefits the object of the act.

In his discussion of *hizmet*, Gülen also echoes the Socratic-Platonic ideal according to which *logos* (a verbal account derived from reason) motivates not just words but *ergon* (action) and *ergon* is undertaken based on *logos*.[147] He was already shaping this philosophy during the early Izmir years and he has subsequently taught and written extensively on it in the years since.

One can recognize a distinct emulation of a *logos-ergon* dynamic in Gülen's assertion that

> "[t]he purpose of our creation is obvious: to reach our utmost goals of belief, knowledge, and spirituality; to reflect on the universe, humanity, and God, and thus prove our value as human beings,"

since he then follows these words with the statement that "[t]hought will provoke action, and thereby start a 'prosperous cycle.'"[148] Thought, words and actions are linked.

More emphatically, the notion of an inherent connection between thought and action for those who truly function as "genuine humans"—as God's vice-regents on earth—is that they "reflect, do what they believe to be right, and then reflect on their behavior."[149] So reflection *on* behav-

---

[147] One among many examples in the Platonic corpus of the relationship between *logos* and *ergon* expressed and enacted by Socrates is found in the *Crito*, in which a wealthy friend of Socrates wishes to spirit him out of prison and away from his imminent execution. Socrates refuses, noting that, as someone who has championed the laws in Athens his entire adult life, and who has pushed again and again for his fellow citizens to keep cross-examining themselves and their putative understandings of law and justice, he could hardly serve as a model to them and to his children if he fled the prison cell and thus disrespected the laws simply because, in human hands, those laws had led to a death-sentence for him. His *ergon* of remaining in prison to face death affirms the *logos* that he delivers to Crito within the dialogue.

[148] "The Meaning of Life," in Section Four ("Sufism and Metaphysics") of *Love and Tolerance*, 219.

[149] Ibid, 220.

ior, like reflection and words that *yield* a particular pattern of behavior, offer the possibility of a reciprocal harmony of the sort that, when realized, yields individuals who most fully express what it means to be *human*. Like Gülen, Socrates and Plato sought this kind of harmony, on behalf of their fellow Athenians.

But of course the specific direction that Gülen's thinking has taken on this matter is different from that articulated by Socrates and Plato. When Gülen reiterates the idea that "our duty is to reflect upon our place in life, our responsibilities, and our relationship with this vast universe..."[150] and that "we [who are] the most important living creations in this universe...should reflect upon and observe the universe so that we may realize and fulfill the purpose of our creation,"[151] he very clearly lifts his ambitions beyond the relatively small world that encompassed Socrates and Plato. Gülen is not focused on a small community such as that of Athens in Socrates' and Plato's day. He attaches reflection and words to actions that focus on and improve the world at large.

Embedding the Socratic-Platonic principle of reflection within a mystical mode, he directly enjoins us to engage in reflection that does not have reflection for its own sake as a goal, but action that, growing out of that reflection, improves the world—which is implied by Socrates/Plato, but not thrust forward. Every action that improves the world improves the reality in which the improver exists. And the key— *hizmet*: service—is the embodiment of actively transforming *logos* into *ergon*.

Where Socrates' Athens-focused frame of reference is governed by spiritual concepts rooted in a belief in diverse and often quarrelsome gods who provide often questionable moral guidance, and whose support of humankind is at times suspect—and certainly not understood as a partnership—Gülen thinks and writes out of a Muslim context in which the world is understood to be guided by a single, all-powerful as well as all-good God who *empowers* humans to continue to shape the moral world in partnership with God. His focus extends beyond

---

[150] Ibid, 220-1.
[151] Ibid, 220-1.

Izmir and beyond Turkey in recognizing that the interwoven quality of the world—particularly in the contemporary world (whether when he was preaching in Izmir in the 1960s or, the more so in writing in Pennsylvania in the internet-dominated world of today)—means that the goal of improving it through *hizmet* must be undertaken on the broadest of scales.[152]

How this has actually played out in Gülen's work and the efforts of those inspired by him during the last four decades and more we shall consider in the chapter that follows.

---

[152] For a fuller discussion of aspects of the relationship between the thinking of Socrates/Plato and Gülen on this subject as well as on education as it is discussed in the following chapter, see Ori Z. Soltes, "Socrates, Violence, Education, the Gülen Movement and Peace," in Soltes, Ori Z. and Margaret Johnson (eds.), *Preventing Violence and Achieving World Peace: Contributions of the Gulen Movement*. (New York, NY: Peter Lang Publishing, 2012). For a fuller discussion of the relationship between the thinking of Socrates/Plato and Gülen as it applies to the *Hizmet* Movement discussed in the next chapter, see Ori Z. Soltes, "Fethullah Gülen and Eco-Justice: From Genesis 1:28 and Qur'an 2:30 to Platonic *ergon* and Aristotelian *harmonia*," in Kim, Heon and John Raines (eds.), *Making Peace*.

Chapter Five

Gülen's Thought as Action: Education and the *Hizmet* Movement

It may be said that Gülen primarily steps beyond the concerns of Rumi or any other Sufi predecessors whom we have considered in the emphasis he places on actively trying to shape a new generation that understands the issues about which he has spent a lifetime teaching and writing and is eager not just to theologize and philosophize but to push for action toward improving the world. One could say that the unique *dhikr* developed by Rumi, which transforms the *verbally* spiritual process—a *sama'*: a *chanted* "concert"—which is the Sufi "norm" into a dynamically *physical* spiritual process has been re-angled by Gülen: *theoretical* and verbally spiritual assertions about human-divine interface and its human-human counterpart are transformed into *actual*, *practical*, and *physically* spiritual deeds.

One could also say that the seeds for transforming thoughts and words into actions that are directed toward serving others and improving the world have also been planted in other Sufi thinkers whose work Gülen has absorbed. Thus earlier we noted how, as al-Qushairi shaped the mystical process into 43 (or 45) stages (*maqamat*) and states (*ahwal*), the *hal* called *irada* ("desire") was referred to by him as the desire to abandon one's *own* desires and do only what God desires, leading to *hurriya* ("magnanimity"). One thereby becomes a *hurr*: one *free* of worldly needs and ecstatically happy to serve others' needs. And beyond these *ahwal*, *jud* and *sakha'* ("generosity" and "givingness") reflect thought and action toward others, inspired by the words of the Prophet that "the giving man is near to God, near to men, near to Paradise, far from Hell."

It is this dictum and its consequences for al-Qushairi's structure that is ultimately articulated and expanded into practical detail by Gülen.[153]

The starting point for this is education for those, young and old—but particularly the young—who would partake in the process of seeking oneness with the One. That search, if successful, will inevitably lead the seeker *back* to a focus on our *own* world and on *how to improve it*. Gülen writes passionately about the importance of educating our children as a means of insuring a better future for the planet—and about the danger to the society that ignores this imperative:

> Children form the most active and productive part of a community after every thirty or forty years. Those who have little children and pay no attention to them should consider how important an element of a people's life they are disregarding and shudder.
>
> ...whatever is spent for the upbringing of young generations to elevate them to the rank of humanity will be like an inexhaustible source of income.[154]

On the one hand, he writes that

> [at] this point, true human progress and evolution in relation to our essential being is only possible with education.[155]

One may recognize as a seed for articulating an education system the words of al-Ghazali that were earlier quoted: "the disciple (*murid*) must of necessity have recourse to a mentor (*shaikh*) to guide him right. For the Path of the faith is obscure, but Iblis's [Satan's] ways are many and potent, and he who has no *shaikh* to guide him will be led by Iblis into *his* ways." The importance of having models to guide one's education is clearly an essential part of the way in which Gülen has advocated for and inspired schools and the educators within them—both as teachers in the classroom and as administrators, so many of whom

---

[153] Gülen discusses many of the specific *maqamat* and *ahwal* delineated in al-Qushairi in his *Key Concepts in the Practice of Sufism: Emerald Hills of the Heart* (Somerset, NJ: The Light, 2006; reprint of 1996 English-language edition of this work).

[154] "Children," in *Criteria*, 54, 55.

[155] "M. Fethullah Gülen on Education," in *Essays—Perspectives—Opinions*, 80.

very clearly demonstrate *hurriya* and other service-directed *ahwal* both within and beyond the classroom itself.

At the same time, one may also recognize as one of Gülen's sources of inspiration in his educational focus and concern, the focus and concern exhibited by Plato in his *Republic*, in which the shaping of an ideal educational program is articulated and in particular the forming of leaders—"guardians" is Plato's term—who will be trained in that program to be shepherds of a state that functions in accordance with the dictates of justice. As "Gülen believes the road to justice for all is dependent on the provision of an adequate and appropriate universal education,"[156] so the relationship between justice and education was first explicitly explored by Plato.

On the other hand, Gülen expands in a less systematic but more broadly-focused and farther-reaching manner than does Plato on the importance of education toward achieving a just society not only within but beyond a given state. He observes of the younger generation, that

> [u]ntil we help them though education, the young are captives of their environment...[157]

and that

> [t]he progress or decline of a nation depends on the spirit and consciousness, the upbringing and education, given to its young.[158]

Moreover, he observes that

> [i]f we do not plant the seeds of love in the hearts of young generations whom we try to revive through sciences, knowledge and modern culture, they will never attain perfection and free themselves completely from the captivation of carnal desires.[159]

So love is an essential message that must be sent to and received by the young who will inherit the world we leave behind, and that mes-

---

[156] "Who is M.Fethullah Gülen?" in Ibid, 5.

[157] "Youth," in *Criteria*, 59.

[158] Ibid, 60.

[159] "Love," in *Criteria*, 30.

sage will be necessary in order for them to recognize the importance of spiritual and not only material elements in and beyond our world. The two obvious questions are: how does Gülen propose to shape that generation beyond his own writing and preaching (particularly when he stopped actively preaching several decades ago)—what sort of system does he offer, and how does it extend beyond what Plato's Socrates lays out in considerable detail in the *Republic*—and what is the course of action that he would wish to see undertaken by those who are subject to it?

For starters, and as a practical matter, in order to assure a balanced sense of the world and eliminate a sense of hierarchical distinction between those with physical skills and those with intellectual skills (for the ideal student develops both):

> ...[T]rades and crafts should be taught beginning at least in the elementary level...[160]

But more fundamentally, how does one go about encouraging a loving sensibility in those whom one is educating? Gülen's view, consistent with his focus on an ongoing relationship between humanity and divinity, is, first of all, that "[t]he best way of equipping one with such values is a sound religious education."[161] More emphatically, education that trains one to function in a proper manner throughout this life also equips one to engage the reality beyond this one. Thus:

> A school is a place of learning about everything related to this life and in the next.... In essence, a school is a kind of place of worship whose "holy people" are teachers...[162] A good lesson is one that does more than provide pupils with useful information or skills; it should elevate them into the presence of the unknown.[163]

But "spiritual" or "religious" should not be confused with narrowly sectarian or divorced from science and its concomitants. Gülen articulates this notion by reference not only to Bediüzzaman Said Nursi,

---

[160] Ibid, 77.
[161] "M. Fethullah Gülen on Education," in *Essays—Perspectives—Opinions*, 76.
[162] Ibid, 76.
[163] Ibid, 78.

but to Albert Einstein, each of whom offers different resonances in his thought.

> As stated by Bediuzzaman, there is an understanding of education that sees the illumination of the mind in science and knowledge, and the light of the heart in faith and virtue... Such an understanding, in Einstein's words, will not allow religion to remain crippled. Nor will it allow religion to be perceived as cut off from intelligence, life, and scientific truth and as a fanatical institution that builds walls between individuals and nations.[164]

Again and again, Gülen underscores the importance of the sciences as part of our educational systems—not in opposition to but in harmony with spirituality. And as he observes that "nature is much more than a heap of material or an accumulation of objects: it has a certain sacredness, for it is an arena in which God's Beautiful Names are displayed,"[165] he reiterates from the angle of evolving an effective system of education the notion that "having dominion" over the earth, "subjecting" it and being "God's vice-regent" over it is not a matter of treating it as a pile of goods for our gratification, but as a sacred expression of God's creative power and presence with which we want (or should want) a strong connection.

Gülen observes not only in broad terms that "[r]eligion guides sciences, determines their real goal, and puts moral and universal human values before sciences as guides," but that a misreading of God's Will—or an abandoning of reflection upon them—can lead and has led not only to "the wars and revolutions of the twentieth century that killed hundreds of millions of people..." but to the problem "...of environmental pollution, which has been caused by scientific materialism...,"[166] which problem humans who function correctly as vice-regents are obligated to try to solve.

---

[164] Ibid, 84. Gülen repeats but slightly expands this paragraph in his essay "Educational Services Are Spreading throughout the World," in Section Six ("Education") of *Love and Tolerance*, 313-14.

[165] Educational Services Are Spreading throughout the World, in Section Six ("Education") of *Love and Tolerance*, 313.

[166] Ibid, 312-13.

Given the expectations of an educational system to "elevate [pupils] into the presence of the unknown,"

> [t]he school must be as perfect as possible with respect to curricu-
> lum, its teacher's scientific and moral standards, and its physical
> conditions. A family must provide the necessary warmth and qual-
> ity of atmosphere in which the children are raised.[167]

Thus ideally, the process of shaping young minds is a partnership between the family and the school—and presumably, if the family falls short, it will fall to the school, fashioned along Gülen-inspired lines, to pick up the slack.

And in spite of the spiritual focus to which Gülen frequently alludes, he is emphatic about also including physical activities, such as sports, in the curriculum, for

> Humans are creatures composed not only of a body and a mind,
> or feelings and spirit; rather, we are harmonious compositions of
> all these elements...
>
> Moreover, each person is a creature made up of feelings that can-
> not be satisfied by the mind, and a creature of spirit; it is through
> the spirit that we acquire our essential human identity.[168]

Thus his prescription is for an educational system that recognizes, appreciates and develops all of the dimensions that define the human being.

The answer to the first question—regarding the shaping of a lov-ing sensibility in those one seeks to educate—is part of the extraordi-nary legacy offered by Gülen to the people inspired by him and, in turn by these altruistic volunteers to the world into which his think-ing has penetrated: schools with an array of directional concerns and pedagogic foci. Schools that will recognize not only the importance for young people of gaining a sense of balance between physical and spiritual aspects of their being but through which such a sense will lead to a balance between who they become and the kind of actions

---

[167] Ibid, 74.
[168] Ibid, 309.

they undertake; that "[t]]here is a mutually supportive and perfective relation between an individual's actions and his inner life..."[169]

Moreover, that inner life is nurtured by a number of kinds of subjects, including the arts—which Plato's ideal school would eschew as too distant from truth, or even deleterious to its pursuit, to be included in his curriculum.[170]

In the fullness of focus on "a perfective relation between an individual's actions and his inner life,"

> In schools, at least as much stress must be laid on good manners as upon other subjects if children are to grow up with sound characters. Education is different from teaching; most human beings can be teachers, but the number of educators is severely limited....[171]

But *education* and not mere teaching and learning is essential to our future since true education is what enables individuals and the societies and cultures of which they are part to grow and improve:

> Education is vital for both societies and individuals. First, our humanity is directly proportional to our emotions' purity.... Second, improving a community is possible by elevating the coming generations to the rank of humanity, not by obliterating the bad ones.[172]

Thus the point of a good educational system is both to allow the best students to flourish and also to elevate the weaker students to higher levels of accomplishment. In that sense, one might argue that his ideas are consonant with those of Plato, albeit without the formally systematized sensibility that would prescribe where those from different strata of society and thus presumed strata of talent would fit so that they might accordingly fit into prescribed strata within society.[173] Further:

---

[169] "The Balance between Physicality and Spirituality," *Criteria*, 80.

[170] Plato's view of the visual arts is that they offer "imitations" of "imitations" of ultimate reality—"Forms/Ideas"—and that poetic arts that show heroes acting unheroically offer poor models for his would-be guardians. See below, fn #187.

[171] "Upbringing," in *Criteria*, 36.

[172] "M. Fethullah Gülen on Education," in *Essays—Perspectives—Opinions*, 71-2.

[173] In the *Republic*, Plato's Socrates prescribes different roles for those from different socio-economic strata within the ideal state he is seeking to shape by way of an ideal

> Although it is fundamental that girls should be brought up to be delicate like flowers and mild and affectionate educator of their children, due attention must also be given to making them inflexible as defenders of truth. Otherwise we shall have transformed them into poor, impotent beings for the sake of delicacy and mildness. We must never forget that a female lion should nevertheless keep the attributes of a lion.[174]

Here Gülen treads a fine line—a treading that further separates him from Plato, for whom women play no such role as seekers (or defenders) of truth—between not ceasing to recognize differences between the genders and the likelihood of diverse roles for young men and women in shaping the world around them, and preparing individuals of both genders to grapple with the world and its issues with equal fervor. But

> ...these new men and women [ie, those who come through the educational programs shaped along Gülenian lines] will be altruists who embrace humanity with love and are ready to sacrifice themselves for the good of others when necessary.[175]

Like the words "love," "compassion," and "tolerance," Gülen often turns to the term "altruism/altruist" to refer to the outcome he seeks for those who become inspired by his words and who pass through the schools that articulate that inspiration in a pedagogic context. This term—referring to one's willingness to do things for others purely in order to do so, as opposed to doing so with the expectation or hope of some sort of recompense beyond the satisfaction of having helped someone else—he treats not only as an *outcome* of love and compassion, but as a *creator* of these sentiments: "Altruism, an exalted human feeling, generates love..."[176]

---

educational system in which those of different strata will be differently trained, from the future guardians down to those on the lowest rungs of the hierarchical ladder.

[174] "Upbringing," in *Criteria*, 37.

[175] "The New Man and Woman," in Section Three ("The Ideal Human") of *Love and Tolerance*, 147.

[176] "The Necessity of Interfaith Dialogue," in *Essays—Perspectives—Opinions*, 49.

An altruistic sensibility is one in which the Socratic sense of *logos* that leads inevitably to *ergon* is fulfilled. The *erga* that are undertaken, moreover, are undertaken not only due to a Socratic sense of it being better to do good acts than to be their recipient (the complement to Socrates' assertions that to know the good is to do the good and that it is worse to harm someone than to be harmed), but even more so, for the sake of the goodness of the actions.

One might say that the altruism that Gülen wants to see emerging in young people is as devoid of self-centeredness as the love that Rabi'a describes as due to God simply because it is God's due. She distinguishes between that sort of pure mystical love and the sort of love given because it satisfies one's self to give it to God. And of course, given both Gülen's multi-valent sources of inspiration and his understanding of all of life—and the ideal educational process—as directed toward God even as that process is also directed to the world that God created, it makes perfect sense that he would prescribe a level of altruism as rarified as Rabi'a's prescription of mystical *mahabba* and wed it to Socrates' emphasis on *logos*-based *erga*.

The point and purpose of following the kind of course of being in the world set forth by Gülen is to yield individuals each of whom may be called a "man of service"—as he terms it in the title to one of his essays. Such an individual

> ......holds everyone in high regard and esteem. He is so balanced and faithful to God's will that he will not turn into idols those whom he praises for their services.... He has to be considerate and fair-minded to everyone who comes to his aid and support the truth.... He is moderate and tolerant when he has taken wing anew and soared to the summits... So sincere and humble that he will never bring to mind all that he has accomplished.[177]

Thus the person of service not only performs services for others in an altruistic manner, s/he acknowledges the *hizmet* of others but in a down-to-earth, matter-of-fact manner: s/he neither expects nor delivers praise for what is, after all, merely engaging in the actions expect-

---

[177] "Man of Service," in *Criteria*, 94–5.

ed of God's vice-regents on the planet, whose goal it is—or ought to be—to improve and perfect the planet for its inhabitants.

Gülen writes of those who have come through the gentle and yet strident process of Gülen-inspired education, who are inexorably drawn forever after to a life of *hizmet*—of serving others—that

> ...if such people can reflect this duty of service and responsibility in the work and service that they carry out, if they are able to pursue the essence of the fundamental principles of existence and obey orders concerning rules of conduct, rather than binding themselves to the consequences of their actions, then any unexpected outcome will not cause them to feel defeated, nor will their enthusiasm wane. Instead, they will carry out all deeds of service with a joy of worship and be aware of the gratitude of having reached the apex of true believers, an apex which is considered to be the highest level of existence.... Such people... rush forward, feeling the intense flavor hidden in the essence of the deed, saying in echo of Rumi:
>
> > *I have become a slave,*
> > *I have become a slave, I have become a slave;*
> > *Slaves are happy when they are set free,*
> > *But I am honored and happy to become a slave.*[178]

Thus the ultimate articulation of this Socratic-Rabi'an principle is offered by Rumi, who perfectly articulates how they become truly free in the servitude toward the world and toward God to which they willingly and lovingly direct and devote themselves. It is difficult to imagine a more appropriate articulation of the paradox endemic to the mystical process than this. And the mystic's obligatory desire to improve the world based on his/her own improved spiritual condition could not be more fundamentally and profoundly emphasized than in this statement of *Hizmet*'s parameters.

Moreover, that sort of Rumi-esque freedom defines the kind of person who completely fulfills the desideratum of *being fully human*:

---

[178] "Humanity and Its Responsiblities," in Section Three ("The Ideal Human") of *Love and Tolerance*, 209–10.

> True freedom, the freedom of moral responsibility, is the distin-
> guishing mark of being human; it motivates and enlivens the con-
> science, and moves aside impediments to the spirit.[179]

And those who have arrived at that sense of freedom, who have removed
the impediments to the spirit through embracing the world of Gülen-
inspired education and through it embracing and thus devoting themselves to the world at large through altruistic *hizmet*, "those who

> have devoted themselves to the bestowal of God's consent and to
> the ideal of loving and being loved by Him... never expect any-
> thing—material or spiritual—in return.... [T]hey devote themselves
> completely to making people love God and to being loved by God,
> dedicating their lives to enlightening others... they avoid divisive
> and antagonistic thoughts such as "they" and "we," "others" and
> "ours."... all they think of is how they can be useful to society and
> how they can avoid disputes with the society of which they are
> members.[180]

Their altruistic impulses are all-embracing, and not limited to members
of one group or another—one faith, one nation, one culture. This is
not to say that Gülen or those he inspired do not or should not take
as a starting point the territory that is most familiar—without a foundation from which to build upon, the edifice of his idealism would be
a castle in the clouds and leave nothing but a trail of *logos* with little
ergon to show for it; *hizmet* would be a discussion point without actualized fulfillment. Thus, in his discussion of "Serving Humanity through
Education" he observes that

> Nations are exactly like next-door neighbors. However, ...national
> existence can be ensured only by protecting each nation's specific
> characteristics... As with all other nations, our essential character-
> istics are religion and language, history and motherland. (84–5)[181]

Moreover,

---

[179] "Freedom," in *Criteria*, 42.
[180] "Spirits Devoted to God," in Section Three ("The Ideal Human") of *Love and Tolerance*, 173-4.
[181] "Serving Humanity through Education," in *Essays—Perspectives—Opinions*, 84–5.

> This path [of life] passes through the inescapable dimension of
> servanthood to God by means of serving, first of all, our families,
> relatives, and neighbors, then our country and nation, and finally
> humanity and creation. This service is our right; conveying it to oth-
> ers is our responsibility.[182]

Thus the beginning point of those naturally closest to us is no more
than a *starting* point: it leads in a series of important concentric circles
outward—as spiritually summarized in the moment described by Bediüzzaman Said Nursi in the Beyazıt Mosque (see above, chapter four,
86–7)—to the serving of not merely humanity but all of creation. And
what we do as a consequence of recognizing the validity and importance
of this process is a privilege. Further, it is a responsibility that, as vice-
regents of Creation, we are ultimately obligated by God to convey to
the next generation that sense of privilege.

And ultimately, the process is one that requires of its nurturers
the same altruistic devotion that they are eager to develop within their
students. Such a process cannot be rushed.

> Patience is of great importance in education. Educating people is
> the most sacred, but also the most difficult task in life... The best
> way to educate people is to show a special concern for every indi-
> vidual, not forgetting that each individual is a different "world."[183]

Moreover, just as Gülen's own *logoi* prescribe a dynamical balance
between thought and action, in the world in which he lives those words
have yielded a diversity of actions—*erga*—that are part of the process
of improving the world, inspired by his *logoi*. Words are of inevitable
importance as instruments for discerning Divine interests and intentions, and reflection is important as a basis for such words. But the
fulfillment of those intentions and the carrying out of those interests is
expressed by the transformation of reflections and words into actions:
erga.

---

[182] Ibid, 90. Gülen repeats this statement, in a somewhat expanded form in his essay
"Schools," in Section Six ("Education") of *Love and Tolerance*, 318–9.

[183] "The School and the Teacher," in "M. Fethullah Gülen on Education," in *Essays—
Perspectives—Opinions*, 77.

And, in fact, the movement that is most often referred to as the Gülen Movement is a movement conceived as one that inherently translates thoughts and words into actions, as we have seen. Thus its proper name is the *Hizmet* Movement.

We may understand *ergon/hizmet* in two ways. The first is the actualization of the educational program such as that envisioned in the previous pages; the second is how those who graduate from such a program go forth into the world and serve it.

One observes the extraordinary datum that, since 1991, hundreds of schools sponsored or inspired by the Gülen Movement, at all educational levels, have opened not only in Turkey, but in the Turkic nations of south central Asia, (27 schools operate in Kazakhstan, for instance), various post-Soviet states, such as Moldavia, Ukraine and Georgia, as well as in western countries such as Australia, Canada, France, Germany, and also the United States. Among recent institutions of higher learning, the Nigerian Turkish Nile University, for example, opened its doors in Abuja, Nigeria on December 9, 2009. This is of considerable significance, considering the record of intolerance and its concomitants in that country: the presence of a Gülen-inspired institution at the university level can and hopefully will have an increasing ripple effect of positive transformation.

One recognizes in this development that the starting point for the establishment of such schools has been Turkey itself, and then in concentric circles their expansion has moved into other Turkic language and culture locales, then locales nearby but beyond the Turkic linguistic and cultural ambit, and then, ultimately, across the planet. This is consistent with Gülen's articulation of beginning the positive processes discussed in previous chapters of this volume "at home" and with an awareness of one's own linguistic, cultural and religious values and identity, but seeking to embrace the world beyond these beginning points.

Moreover, from the elementary to the university level, thousands of students, across national, ethnic and religious boundaries study an extended array of disciplines: science, mathematics, history, language, literature, social and cultural studies, art, music and sports. The curric-

ulum at all levels is designed to consider the intellectual and emotional development of students, as well as their physical development.[184]

In writing about education as an essential component within his
thinking about improving the world, Gülen refers to a comment written by a journalist, Ali Bayramoğlu, in the aftermath of having visited
a good number of Gülen-inspired schools. Bayramoğlu writes:

> Those schools don't give religious education or encompass education-
> al activities with a religious environment, as it is assumed. They have
> been established on the model of Anadolu high schools,[185] with
> superior technical equipment and laboratories. Lessons are given with-
> in the curriculum prepared by the Ministry of National Education.
> Religious subjects are not even taught... Activities take place with-
> in the framework of each country's current laws and educational
> philosophy... Giving religious knowledge or religious education is
> not the goal.[186]

This description offers two of the essential aspects of Gülen-inspired
educational thinking. It places science and contemporary technical
skills in the forefront of the process. Further, by excluding formal religious instruction (but not *moral, values*-laden instruction—instruction
directed to the shaping of the spirit, just not the sort of specific instruction associated with *madrasa*s or other similar kinds of sectarian institutions) from the curriculum—and conforming to the specific educational philosophy of the place where the school is located—it is implicitly
(and in fact, explicitly) open to students of all religious backgrounds.

That non-denominational emphasis and the effort to gear the
curriculum to the place where the school is located are also noted by
Father Thomas Michel, General Secretary of the Vatican Secretariat

---

[184] Thus for instance, Fatih University outside Istanbul includes Faculties of Engineering,
Economics and Administrative Sciences, Law, Medicine, Arts and Sciences as well
as Vocational Training; within the arts and Sciences, available departments in six
different language and literature concentrations as well as departments that range
from Biology and Chemistry to Psychology and Sociology. There is a wide array of
cultural and sports activities, and 71 student clubs and groups, with a strong emphasis on multi-culturalism.

[185] Anadolu schools are state-run schools in which scientific subjects are taught in
English.

[186] "Education from Cradle to Grave," in *Essays—Perspectives—Opinions*, 88–9.

for Inter-religious Dialogue in an essay first delivered as a conference paper, in 2001:

> I had expected to find a more explicitly Islamic curriculum, but this was not the case. When I asked about the surprising absence of what to me would have been an understandable part of a religiously-inspired educational project, I was told that because of the pluralistic nature of the student bodies—Christian and Muslim in Zamboanga, and Buddhist and Hindu as well in Kyrghizstan—that what they sought to communicate were universal values such as honesty, hard work, harmony, and conscientious service rather than any confessional instruction.[187]

This more of education could not be more exemplary of the viewpoint famously expressed in Rumi's exhortation:

> Come, come wherever you are.
> Wanderer, worshipper, lover of leaving, it doesn't matter...[188]

Nonetheless, "[i]nitially, some of our foreign affairs officials were hesitant to give their support for they did not really understand what was going on. Today, however, most of them support the schools."[189] That is, these officials mistook the Gülen-inspired schools for Islamist indoctrination centers, whereas they have proven to be centers, simply, of intense, high-energy learning that are not only open to all but provide a broad and deep education that encourages inquiry, discussion, debate—in short, reflection and thought—and inspiration to *hizmet*-centered action that spills inevitably back into the communities from which the students come, to everybody's benefit.

In Turkey, their curricula must and do conform to the secular state's prescriptions—but they stand out in that their students consis-

---

[187] Thomas Michel, "Gülen as Educator and Religious Teacher," in "What Others Say about M.Fethullah Gülen," in *Essays—Perspectives—Opinions*, 106. Father Michel first delivered this essay as a paper at the F. Gülen Symposium at Georgetown University, in April, 2001. Zamboanga is on the southern Philippine island of Mindanao, which he had first visited in 1995.

[188] These lines are extracted from a slightly larger poem inscribed on Rumi's tomb in Konya, Turkey.

[189] "Educational Services Are Spreading throughout the World," in Section Six ("Education") of *Love and Tolerance*, 318.

tently finish at the very top of the Turkish student population according
to every standard of measure applied by the state—so that, although
impelled as Gülen is by Islam, the schools are not platforms from
which, per se, to preach Islam along any lines at all, much less along
particularized lines of this or that ideology. [190] It is such an extraordinary and consistent pattern of success that has led to the enthusiastic
embrace of such schools not only within Turkey but well beyond that
nation's borders.

Their universalist, non-sectarian modus operandi and appeal can
be felt virtually wherever such schools take shape.

> In fact, speaking at the opening ceremonies for the school in
> Moscow, the Head of the Moscow National Education Office said:
> "There are two important events in Russia's recent history. One of
> these is Gagarin's journey to the skies. The other is the opening of a
> Turkish school here." He described this as an historic event. [191]

That stunning reference, let us not forget, comes from the capital of
the state that, since 1917 or so has not only been the ultimate Com-
munist—secularist, religion-denying and hostile to religion—nation,
but also a nation that has been struggling for nearly two decades in a
terrorism-laced relationship with the Muslim Chechnyan people. It is
hardly the atmosphere in which a Gülen-inspired school could gain

---

[190] Thus Gülen's vision extends beyond Plato with respect to what constitutes an ideal
education system as delineated by the latter (with Socrates as his mouthpiece) in
his *Republic*. Plato, for example, would eliminate subjects in the arts that, for various reasons he deems detrimental to the training of his leaders, the Guardians.
Thus passages in the *Iliad*, for instance, that represent Achilles as a cry-baby after
having been insulted by Agamemnon (discussed in *Republic* 387e8-388d1); or the
visual arts, which, he believed, offered mere imitation of reality—which is itself merely
an imitation of the "Forms"/"Ideas" (*Republic* 596b1-598c2)—would not be part
of his curriculum. But the Gülen-inspired educational system emphatically includes
the arts, which are recognized as an essential part of shaping a multi-dimensional
human being. Even poetry or prose that offers unheroic-behaving heroes can help
the student to consider what it is that *makes* a human being heroic—what it is that
makes a genuine, ideal human being; and visual art doesn't *imitate* reality but *re-
visions and transforms* it through the mind of the artist, creating something with its
own validity and not merely offering a pale reflection of objective reality.
[191] "Educational Services Are Spreading throughout the World," in Section Six
("Education") of *Love and Tolerance*, 318.

traction, much less such lavish praise, if it were other than a fulfillment of the universalist educational ideas and ideals espoused by Gülen, in which each such school becomes a laboratory for interaction among its diverse students.

Clearly the student body will vary, depending upon its location and demographics, which makes such a school very much like the ideal American public school. Perhaps the difference is that Gülen-inspired schools actually realize that ideal, which may not as easily be said for an enormous number of American public schools. This is possible, simply, because the Gülen-inspired schools consistently combine first-rate equipment and a first-rate curriculum with a dedicated, first-rate faculty.[192] The closest models to these in the United States are certain private schools (many of which, however, are not non-denominational) and more recently, charter schools. Not surprisingly, Gülen-inspired administrators and faculty in the U.S. are most often drawn to the shaping of charter schools, and are in any number of locations transforming difficult "inner city" school populations into models of achievement.[193]

Indeed, from Turkey itself to Central Asia, Europe and Africa to America, students studying at Gülen-inspired schools are provided with teachers of exemplary dedication, curricula of profound quality and ambitious range—and an embracing vision that looks to global betterment through the teaching of tolerance of difference and the embrace of dialogue.[194] More significantly, perhaps, it is most often the case, as time moves on, that former students become teachers in these

---

[192] This last comment is based both on my reading and the discussion in essays such as Gülen's "Education from Cradle to Grave," in *Essays—Perspectives—Opinions*; and from visits to Gülen-inspired schools and/or discussions with students and teachers in such schools in Turkey (in and around Istanbul) and the United States (in and around Philadelphia) in 2009 and 2010.

[193] This last comment also derives, in part, from discussions with faculty and administrators in the Philadelphia area in November, 2010.

[194] I am also asserting this based not only on book-research, but on the experience of having visited a number of Gülen Movement schools in August, 2009 and having had the opportunity to speak with administrators, teachers and students at several different grade levels.

schools, and their interest and commitment—their dedication to promoting the encompassing principles espoused by the *Hizmet* Movement—are palpable. They teach, in fact, by example: their *logoi* are consistently demonstrated by their *erga*. They are, therefore, part of the embodiment of the second aspect of the *ergon/hizmet* principle: they live lives consistent with what they teach and, at a basic level, their devotion to their teaching is measurable by their willingness to put in far more than the "ordinary" classroom hours to help their students grow.

Thus both those who teach and those who study in the Gülen Movement schools are in the process of embracing and expressing and/ or learning to embrace a three-fold (intellectual, spiritual/emotional,[195] physical) mode of engaging each other and the world. They embrace the importance of *hizmet* as a centerpiece in that engagement, the point and purpose of which is to become leaders who help improve the world—to have dominion and be divinely ordained vice-regents in the sense addressed in the various essays by Gülen to which this discussion of his thinking has referred.

The pattern of *hizmet* extends beyond the Ivory Tower in two ways. One is that the funding for the well-equipped schools that are able to offer their students such an array of educational opportunities is facilitated entirely through the contributions of those who, inspired by the teachings of Fethullah Gülen, want to see his principles further promoted within the world at large. The schools are privately run and administered, even as all of their facets strictly follow the educational guidelines but typically exceed the expectational parameters of the state in which they are located.

The second *hizmet* extension carries beyond the schools into other domains that are positioned to offer both Gülen's ideas of universal benevolence (in the original Latin-based sense of "doing good") and the consequences of those ideas for the world at large. Thus the Gülen Movement extends a web of discussion by means of media of diverse sorts, from paper-based to electronic–based modes of communication.

---

[195] The spiritual is, to repeat, not specifically Islamic; it is directed toward developing "good characters through an emphasis on good manners" and instilling good, service-directed values through providing dedicated models.

Newspapers, journals and books offer one outlet for extending both education and the discourse toward which education ideally pushes us; a varied range of cable and internet programming extends the potential web of dialogue around the globe.[196]

A growing array of fora has spread both the interest in and development of distinguished programs of discussion, dialogue and concern for the world in its diversity and its varied issues and complications. These fora are named for Rumi, and inspired by the inclusive, universalist principles that he articulates, which are championed by Gülen. These "Rumi Fora" are also inspired by Gülen himself; again and again, on their own and in concert with other groups and organizations, they sponsor myriad conferences, symposia, lectures and discussions. They are the proof of the feasibility of seeking peace along the broadest of lines through dialogue.[197]

---

[196] Thus, for example, *The Journalists and Writers Foundation*, which is an extended forum directed "Towards Universal Peace;" publications such as *Zaman* newspaper, and the just-referenced and broadly-focused journal, *The Fountain: A Magazine of Scientific and Spiritual Thought*; and an extensive and varied cable programming channel, *Ebru* TV, that offers programs on a virtually infinite variety of subjects intended to offer viewers with information and food for thought.

[197] In early 2010 alone, consider the following array of topics presented by the Rumi Forum, Washington, DC, some of them sponsored by the Forum itself and some of it co-sponsored with other organizations: "Shalom/Salaam: the Story of a Mystical Fraternity," with Tom Block; "Healing the Family of Abraham," with Joseph V. Montville; "Why Russia Matters: U.S. Russian Relations in the Obama Administration," with Ambassador James F. Collins; "Religion Builds Peace in the Holy Land," with Dr. Yehudah Stolov; "Recent Elections in Afghanistan and its Potential Impact on the Region," with J. Alexander Thier; "China and the Muslim Peoples of the Middle East," with Ambassador Chas W. Freeman, Jr.; "Global Financial Crisis and US-Turkish Trade Opportunities," with Congressman Gregory Meeks; "Stories from Afghanistan," with Dr Nancy Gallagher; "Beyond Fundamentalism: Confronting Extremism in the Age of Globalization," with Dr. Reza Aslan.

This is just a random and certainly abbreviated sampling of the large number and wide range of programs. I might add that in the greater Washington, DC area there are no less than three Rumi Forum organizations. The above programs were sponsored by the Rumi Forum in downtown Washington. A second, centered at the University of Maryland offers its own programs and conferences. The spiritually tri-lateral members of the third, at Georgetown University, were engaged, through all of 2009 and much of 2010, in a group study and discussion of eschatology in the Abrahamic traditions.

Dialogue throughout this narrative and throughout Gülen's writings, pertains essentially to discussions across faith borders that will lead to greater interfaith understanding—stemming from love, compassion and tolerance and in turn leading to love, compassion and tolerance—that is an essential part of the Gülen *logos* of how to be in the world, and which thus inherently leads beyond *logos* to *ergon* which, as *hizmet*, serves the world. It furthers, on a practical level what is implied in the myriad statements by Rumi and others, like Ibn al-'Arabi, who, important to the development of Gülen's own thinking, have proclaimed themselves at one with the world in all of its diverse faith-bound and even faithless parts. But it is also a methodology of trying to get closer to the truth, as articulated in the beginnings of Western thought, and shaped and nurtured, by Socrates and Plato.

In Socrates' and Plato's terms, dialogue is opposed, as a methodology for pursuing truth, to the method of working alone: two or more minds engaged together in inquiry—what is Virtue? Piety? Courage? Truth?—as opposed to one mind on its own. The term that they used of the process—*elenkhos*, in Greek—means "cross-examination." Every concept that is considered, however it is defined, finds its definition wrestled with, back and forth, between or among the discussants, as they seek to refine their understanding in an ongoing, very active intellectual process.

Gülen's important understanding of, and his intellectual relationship with, the thinking of Socrates reflects a sense of an intimate relationship between justice and education, on the one hand, and between training individuals at every level within a society to contribute toward its perfection *as* just, on the other. It is part of what he articulates as the best way to fulfill being human in being in the world.

> ...Those individuals who are sufficient to themselves, disconnected from others and unconcerned with their opinions, even if they happen to be geniuses, are at considerable risk of error compared to those who offer and receive opinions in consultation.

> Consultation is the first condition for obtaining good results...
> ...Two lots of knowledge are better than one.[198]

Thus it is no surprise to find dialogue as a layered concept reflected in the range of educational and other institutions inspired by him and popularly associated with his name (though he is emphatic—repeatedly—about not attributing all these institutions and their "divinely granted" achievements to him), that encourage thinking individuals to think and reflect as well as to speak and to act.

With inputs across centuries and cultures, from Socrates to Nursi, Gülen has constructed an idealist's vision with two features that idealist's visions more often than not lack: millions of individuals who have been inspired to follow the lead that he has offered in preachings and teachings and writings for nearly half a century; and concrete realizations of that vision in myriad ways across the planet.

Those inspired by him are in the gradual process of being part of the solution to the problems that continue to shape too much of the world. That process seeks to champion the cause of culture and civilization. The first of these terms, as Gülen defines it, offers, for each particularized culture, a sense of its distinct part within a greater whole and of the importance of both the part and the whole. For

> A people can keep distinctive culture only by making a harmonious composition from their religious and moral values and human virtues and knowledge.[199]

The second, civilization, simply "means being civil and courteous, kind-hearted, profound in thought and respectful to others."[200] His interest, like that of Jalaluddin Rumi, is to help shape an all-embracing, *universalist* civilization in which each particular sectarian *part* enjoys a strong sense of its own identity and also a love of and compassion and tolerance toward other parts with their own identities. This is a combination that seeks to promote a universal harmony.

---

[198] "Consultation," in *Criteria*, 39. I have reversed the order of the last two lines.
[199] "Culture," in *Criteria*, 47.
[200] "Civilization," in *Criteria*, 49.

Chapter Six

Between Past and Future:
Gülen's Vision, Its Sources and Goals:
In Pursuit of a Better World

In the purest sense of the word, Gülen may be considered a *jiha-dist*—in the true meaning and not the common parlance misunderstanding of that word. The Arabic term *jihad*, properly translated and understood, means "struggle." The primary sense of that term is the obligation of every Muslim to struggle to be a better Muslim—one who submits and surrenders to God's will. As Gülen explains:

> Islam is a word derived from the root words *silm* and *salamah*. It means surrendering, guiding to peace and contentment, and establishing security and accord.[201]

Thus the surrendering of one's self to God's will is to commit one's self to bringing peace and contentment not only to one's self, but to others. Indeed, the secondary sense of *jihad* is to struggle to shape the Muslim world—the *umma*—as a more effective realm of submission to God's will. The tertiary sense pertains to improving the world at large to a condition of submission to God's will.

Gülen himself, as a scholar of the Qur'an and hadith and the sweep of Muslim literature and lore, writes extensively on this term, with the distinct intention of disabusing both Muslims and non-Muslims of the notion that the tertiary meaning of *jihad* is primary and/or that such a

---

[201] "Islam—A Religion of Tolerance," in Section Two ("Forgiveness, Tolerance and Dialogue") of *Love and Tolerance*, 111.

meaning necessarily connotes violence.[202] To begin with, he points out an important distinction:

> The internal struggle (the greater *jihad*) is the effort to attain one's essence; the external struggle (the lesser *jihad*) is the process of enabling someone else to obtain his or her essence. The first one is based on overcoming obstacles between oneself and one's essence... The second is based on removing obstacles between people and faith so that people can choose freely between belief and unbelief. In one respect, *jihad* is the purpose of our creation and our most important duty...[203]
>
> ...in short, everything is done for God's sake—and regulating love and anger according to His approval is included. In this way all efforts made to reform society and people are part of *jihad*, as is every effort made for your family, relatives, neighbors, and region.
>
> In a sense, the lesser *jihad* is material. The greater *jihad*, however, is conducted on the spiritual front, for it is our struggle with our inner world and carnal soul (*nafs*). When both of these *jihad*s have been carried out successfully, the desired balance is established.[204]

Thus the preponderant meaning of the term has to do with one's own desire to function in a manner pleasing to God, to make the utmost effort to please God and to help—not to force—others to do the same. To help them not to accord with your own vision and interpretation of what God is but their own—or to struggle in a pure, intellectual manner, a manner that is part of what in the previous chapter of this volume was referred to in Gülen's terms as "consultation"— and in Socrates/Plato's terms as *elenkhos*.

---

[202] When Gülen uses the term "*jihad*," he typically does not italicize it, nor do his translators. I prefer to do so, in order to emphasize for my reader that the term is not to be taken as a word that has entered the English vernacular as an easily recognized, everyday term: although that may actually be so, too often the term is misconstrued—usually to mean "holy war"—and my use of italics is intended to cause the reader to pause and consider the real meanings of the term whenever s/he encounters it in this narrative (and hopefully elsewhere as well).

[203] "Lesser and Greater Jihad," in Section Five ("Jihad—Terrorism and Human Rights") of *Love and Tolerance*, 276-7.

[204] Ibid, 278.

It is all done for God's sake and the primary distinction is not between *jihad* within my own soul and *jihad* for or on behalf of someone else's soul, or within and on behalf of my community's soul—but between spiritual and material *jihad*. And the fully realized human being, who recognizes his or her role as a representative of creation, who is imbued with love and compassion, tolerance and respect for others, regardless of the particulars of their understanding of the universe and the God beyond it Who created it—that individual has achieved a dynamic equilibrium between greater and lesser, spiritual and material *jihad*:

> Believers find peace and vitality in such a balanced *jihad*. ...[T]hose who pursue *jihad* are always surrounded by love and enthusiasm. Their inner worlds are bright, their feelings are pure, and they are on the road to prosperity. Every struggle stimulates the thought of yet another one and thus a righteous circle is formed. As every good deed becomes a vehicle for a new good deed, such people swim among good deeds.[205]

Gülen pursues his distinction between greater and lesser *jihad*, emphasizing a Sufi perspective that would have found an unequivocal resonance for Rumi as well as for Rabi'a, Ibn al-'Arabi, Bediüzzaman Said Nursi and other Sufis:

> The lesser *jihad* is our active fulfillment of Islam's commands and duties; the greater *jihad* is proclaiming war on our ego's destructive and negative emotions and thoughts (e.g., malice, hatred, envy, selfishness, pride, arrogance, and pomp), which prevent us from attaining perfection...[206]

The goal of the Sufi, the mystic, is to be filled with God by finding the hiddenmost recesses of God—the *mysterion*—both far outside herself (*ecstasy*) or deep within himself where the fragment of God that *is* each of our souls resides, from the moment we are born (*enstasy*). In order to accomplish this, mystics must transcend and abandon them-

---

[205] Ibid, 278.
[206] Ibid, 279.

selves, so that the soul-space filled by self will be filled, instead, with the knowledge-beyond-normative-knowledge and love of God.

To succeed in accomplishing this is to succeed in the most perfect of *jihads*—the sort of *jihad* that emphatically precludes violence toward anyone but includes the loving, compassionate desire to return from that condition of *enstasy/ecstasy* in an enlightened condition through which one may improve the world. It would seem obvious that

> [t]hose who succeed in the greater *jihad* will succeed in the lesser *jihad*; those who fail in the greater *jihad* will fail in the lesser *jihad*. Even if such people obtain some degree of success, they cannot obtain full results.[207]

Jihad as struggle, then, by no means implies violent struggle. Even when "*Jihad* can be a matter of self-defense or of removing obstacles between God and human free choice,"[208] the intention of the term is to remove the mental and spiritual obstructions that prevent one from realizing human free will within the context of a universe engendered by an all-powerful, all-knowing, loving God. If "self-defense" implies physical violence, then such action is embraced only as a last resort—not when one is failing to convince someone of one's spiritual point of view, but because one's life is threatened.

At various times and places the term *jihad* has been reduced in understanding to its tertiary meaning—struggle in the world at large and *with* the world at large toward its Islamicization in the specific, narrow sense—by speakers of the term or practitioners of what they believe to be the concept. Such an understanding has further been understood to justify violence as a means of accomplishing God's will. But that meaning and that understanding are emphatically rejected by Gülen, as they have been rejected by key Muslim thinkers—notably Rumi—who have inspired him. Gülen repeatedly "describes those who resort to force as being intellectually bankrupt…"[209]

---

[207] Ibid, 279.

[208] "Islam: A Religion of Tolerance," in Section Two (Forgiveness, Tolerance and Dialogue), of *Love and Tolerance*, 112.

[209] "Who is M. Fethullah Gülen?" in M Fethullah Gülen, *Essays, Perspectives, Opinions*, 5. As a practical matter, Gülen was one of the first Muslim leaders to speak out

He observes, simply:

> There is no room for hate or hostility in either Islam or in the uni-
> versal realms of its envoy Muhammad, peace and blessings be upon
> him.[210]

Thus his thinking along these lines not only sees violence as the wrong
solution to the problem of insufficient adherence to God's will. He recognizes that "God's will" is a finely nuanced one, requiring constant
examination and re-examination to fathom. *Jihad* is the sort of struggle
that, through such constant examination and re-examination, seeks to
provide its examiners with the instruments to fulfill that will. But as
humans are endlessly multifarious, the interpretive conclusions that they
will draw from their examinations will vary.

Jihad means not only to struggle within one's self but to struggle
with the ways in which others will arrive at slightly different conclusions regarding God's will, and to struggle to integrate diverse views
into a comprehensive whole that will provide society with justice for
its constituents. Gülen's thought on this matter offers part of his relationship with Socratic *elenkhos*—cross-examination—the purpose of
which, in Socratic/Platonic contexts, is to arrive at definitions of terms
and ideas, like "justice," "piety" and "virtue," that we find difficult or
perhaps even impossible to define. For Gülen the indefinable terms are
God, God's Will and how human action may function as an agent of
that Will to promote justice and virtue in a world in which God has
declared humans to be His vice-regents.[211]

Moreover, Gülenian *jihad*—Gülenian struggle—accords very well
with the sort of struggle expressed in Socratic-Platonic thought when,
in referring to the process of *elenkhos*, Plato's Socrates speaks of a birth-

---

loudly, clearly and unequivocally in the aftermath of the September 11 attacks as
both outrageous and non-Islamic: His press release at that time noted succinctly
that "[a] terrorist cannot be a Muslim and a Muslim cannot be a terrorist." But his
anti-violence perspective long pre-dates 2001.

[210] "Real Muslims Cannot Be Terrorists," in Section Five ("Jihad—Terrorism and Human
Rights") of *Love and Tolerance*, 291.

[211] ™ ˌ initial Qur'anic reference to this role for humans is found in Q 2:30. See above,
ˋ6.

ing process effected by dialogue in which both dialogue and Socrates himself are referred to as midwives of ideas. The pain of perplexity occasioned by the realization that concepts we thought we grasped without thinking about what they really mean is likened to a birthing pain—that yields the progeny of true knowledge and wisdom. And it yields, moreover, a better world when the process is harnessed to an altruistic sense of *ergon-hizmet*.

At the same time we may see in Gülen's thought yet another important departure from the thinking of Socrates' pupil, Plato. For Plato ultimately turned against democracy as a political mechanism, discouraged by its failures from appreciating its value. The irony is that the very issue that Gülen emphasizes—freedom in expressing spiritual and religious values—was in the end denied in the Athenian democracy that executed Socrates on religious grounds, and it was the decision to execute Socrates that turned Plato against the idea of regarding democracy.

Gülen, drawing from other sources and his own relationship to the world, sees democracy as the primary means of assuring the religious freedom that he deems so essential to a better world. He asserts that "people will always demand freedom of choice in the way they run their affairs and in their expression of their spiritual and religious values. Democracy, Gülen argues, in spite of its many shortcomings, is now the only viable political system."[212]

It is along the lines of this divergence from Plato's political philosophy that Gülen's vision of Platonic dialogue is constructed. His interest is not merely in seeking to understand truth and a host of other ideas through the process of dialogue as an educational mechanism. Gülen thinks simultaneously on a more fundamental level about the importance of dialogue as a mechanism of communication among adherents of different faiths. The intention of such dialogue is not to prove the superiority of one faith over another but, in mutual respect for the Rumi-esque realization that all true faiths can lead to the same *mysterion* within God, to channel the energies of interfaith dialogue toward

---

[212] "Who is M. Fethullah Gülen?" in M Fethullah Gülen, *Essays, Perspectives, Opinions*, 5.

deeper mutual respect and love, compassion and tolerance, in the sense of *embrace*:

> Interfaith dialogue is a must today, and the first step in establishing it is forgetting the past, ignoring polemical arguments, and giving precedence to common points, which far outnumber polemical ones. (38)

Most fundamentally, that dialogue is both necessary and possible as Gülen understands it, because those who will engage in it—those like Rumi and other Sufis, form Rabi'a to Nursi—have, as a starting point, a love of God and thus a desire to improve the world because that improvement process is a way of expressing that love and of seeking to fulfill the condition of being, on a microcosmic scale, a reflection of the manifestations of God, the ultimate and consummate macrocosmic bringer into being of order.

> ... Above all else, a believer must love Him, and have a liking for all others only because they are colorful manifestations and reflections of His Divine Names and Attributes. Also, people must applaud these things with great admiration, and each time a person sees such a thing s/he must think, "This too, is by You," and experience a period of unification with the Lover. For this, however, we need pure and virtuous people that can read the verses of God in the faces of people. Verily, for those who can decipher, every creature is a shining mirror and a eulogy written in great verse; above all else is the human face, reflecting the secret of Mercy.

> *The All-just made you a mirror of His Self,*
> *A mirror of His Unique Self*
>
> Hakani[213]

This is the vision of humanity that Fethullah Gülen possesses, promotes and to which he repeatedly refers. It is the vision that he sees as paramount within the Islam that he embraces and within the humanity that he embraces. Humans are, ideally,

---

[213] "Love of God," in Section One ("Love and Mercy") of *Love and Tolerance*, 49. The couplet he quotes is from Hakani Mehmed Bey (d. 1606), a divan poet whose *Hilya* (a verbal portrait delineating the qualities of the Prophet Muhammad) was the first of its kind.

the greatest mirror of the names, attributes and deeds of God, …a shining mirror, a marvelous fruit of life, and a source for the whole universe, a sea that appears to be a tiny drop, a sun formed as a humble seed, a great melody in spirit of their insignificant physical positions, and the source for existence all contained within a small body. Humans carry a holy secret that makes them equal to the entire universe with all their wealth of character; a wealth that can be developed to excellence.[214]

It is through recognizing this and realizing how diverse human intellectual and spiritual inclinations can interweave each other that we can strive most effectively to perfect the world. We are poised in the world that Gülen describes and prescribes to transcend the antagonisms that, in the past, have held us back from that goal.

> Previous generations witnessed a bitter struggle that should never have taken place: science versus religion. This conflict gave rise to atheism and materialism, which influenced Christianity more than other religions. Science cannot contradict religion, for its purpose is to understand nature and humanity, which are a composition of the manifestations of God's Attributes of Will and Power… Thanks to the efforts of both Christian and Muslim theologians and scientists, it seems that the religion-science conflict that has lasted for a few centuries will come to an end, or at least its absurdity will finally be acknowledged.[215]

Moreover, as with Gülen's turning of the issue of dialogue in a specifically interdenominational direction, his sense of how science and religion must interweave can also interweave the working of Western and Eastern sensibilities—in a manner that can offer hope for emerging from the sort of human-made catastrophes that have defined the twentieth and early twenty-first centuries:

> It has always been possible for peoples who combine science with morality to found true civilizations. For this reason, Western civilization has always remained paralyzed since it has been based main-

---

[214] "Human Beings and Their Nature," in Section Three ("The Ideal Human") of *Love and Tolerance*, 190.

[215] "At the Threshold of a New Millennium," in Section Seven ("Global Perspectives") of *Love and Tolerance*, 363.

ly upon science only. On the other hand, Eastern civilizations are far from being true since, in their present conditions, they are devoid of any scientific background. The civilization of the future will have to be founded upon a combination of Western sciences and Eastern faith and morality.[216]

It is in responding to this sensibility that we can indeed fulfill the sort of role defined in both the Qur'an and the Hebrew Bible for humanity, not only vis-à-vis itself and each other, but vis-a-vis the planet at large, to be stewards and guardians of all the elements of creation. For, those termed by Gülen "people of faith" recognize that "[o]ur duty is to reflect upon our place in life, our responsibilities, and our relationship with this vast universe."[217] They understand that

> [t]he purpose of our creation is obvious: to reach our utmost goals of belief, knowledge, and spirituality; to reflect on the universe, humanity and God, and thus prove our value as human beings. [And they understand that f]ulfilling this ideal is possible only through systematic thinking and systematic behavior. Thought will provoke action, and thereby start a "prosperous cycle"...[218]

Such individuals

> feel the vastness of the title of vicegerent which has been bequeathed to them.... They sip water, breath air and accept all manners of presents as blessings from God. They inhale the scent of the Earth and those that it gives birth to as if it were the sweetest of aromas. They salute the orchards and gardens, the mountains and valleys, the grasses and trees, the roses and the flowers with the language of their heart, as if these things too had senses.They caress all creatures that they encounter as if they were friends assigned to keep them company in this guesthouse. With every action they demonstrate that they have been sent to the Earth as a sign for agreement and reconciliation.[219]

---

[216] "Civilization," in *Criteria*, 49–50.

[217] "The Meaning of Life," in Section Four ("Sufism and Metaphysics") of *Love and Tolerance*, 220.

[218] Ibid, 219.

[219] "The Horizons of Tranquility," in Section Four ("Sufism and Metaphysics") of *Love and Tolerance*, 261–2. For a more detailed discussion of Gülen and eco-justice, see Ori Z. Soltes, "Fethullah Gülen and Eco-Justice: From Genesis 1:28 and Qur'an

Indeed, when we transform theory into action,

> [t]here is no limit of goodness that can be done for others. Those
> who dedicate themselves to doing good for humanity are so altru-
> istic that they can even sacrifice their lives for others. However such
> altruism is a great virtue only if it originates in sincerity and purity
> of intention; it should be far removed from racial or tribal super-
> stitions.[220]

When acts of altruism are real—when they do originate in sincerity and
purity of intention—then the path toward perfecting the world becomes
clearer. Our duty as a species becomes clearer:

> ...[O]ur essential duty as a creation that has come to this passing
> guesthouse with a pure nature is to reach stability and clarity in
> thought, imagination, and belief so that we can acquire a "second
> nature" and qualify to continue our life in "the next, much more
> elevated realms."[221]

Speaking out of an Islamic frame of reference, Gülen observes, in one
of his more felicitous observations:

> The universe is just a large Qur'an that has been physically created
> by God for our instruction. In return, as it is an expression of the
> laws of the universe in yet another form, the Qur'an is a universe
> that has been codified and written down.[222]

Thus the microcosm of God's word through Prophet Muhammad
and the macrocosm of the universe engendered by God are echoed in
each other; to study either is to open the door to study both. But how
does this encompass those whose primary God-revealed text is other
than the Qur'an, such as the Hebrew Bible or the New Testament? The
answer becomes obvious, when we come full circle to consider the
mystical—Sufi—roots of so much of Gülen's thinking. All paths lead

---

2:30 to Platonic *ergon* and Aristotelian *harmonia*," in Kim, Heon and John Raines
(eds), *Making Peace*.

[220] "Real Life and Real Humanity," in Section Seven ("Global Perspectives") of *Love
and Tolerance*, 343.

[221] "Educational Services are Spreading Throughout the World," in Section Six
("Education") in *Love and Tolerance*, 311.

[222] Ibid, 312.

to the same goal, when travelled with sincerity of intent motivated by love, compassion, tolerance and altruistic *hizmet*.

Mysticism in the Abrahamic traditions in particular is inherently paradoxic. It asserts the possibility of having intimate contact—interweaving one's very soul, one's essence—with a God that is both already with us and yet inconceivably different from and distant from us, unattainable and inaccessible. It demands that we empty ourselves of *self* in order to be filled with the love of God and that our desire for intimacy with God come from an entirely selfless desire to improve the condition of the world, as opposed to having as a goal simply to gain enlightenment for ourselves (which would be *selfish*, signifying that our selves are too *full* of self to make room for God). It requires a transcendence of *sense*, in order to achieve that hoped-for intimacy with the God beyond sense.

Within Jewish and Muslim mysticism, the notion that there is a hiddenmost recess to God—a *mysterion*—would imply some concept of inner and outer that seems, by normative logic, to impute to God spatiality and duality, which notions are rigorously opposed by the normative logic of the Jewish and Muslim understanding of God as incontrovertibly One, singular, and without any sense-related attributes that would impose any spatial considerations whatsoever upon Divinity. So the very underlying enterprise of seeking access to the *mysterion* within the One is inherently paradoxic within these two traditions.[223]

Within the context of such profoundly perfect illogic, it is supremely logical that a consummate mystic such as Jalaluddin Rumi, as a Sufi steeped within his own Muslim tradition, and using that tradition as his foundation and the beginning point of his search for spiritual intimacy with the One should, as much as he seeks that intimacy through the exclusive lens of *that* tradition, at the same time be emphatically all-embracing. For the insight he has received from the

---

[223] Given its innately paradoxic understanding of God as triune, whereby the three aspects of Godness can and cannot be distinguished, and in which one of those aspects takes human form as Jesus of Nazareth, Christianity is in its mainstream mode, inherently paradoxic and mystical, and in its mystical mode not inherently disturbed by the inner-outer paradox that disturbs Judaism and Islam.

mysterion is distinctly that, if and when it is reached, it may be reached from an infinite number of directions.[224]

It is this realization that causes Rumi to open his spiritual arms to all so consistently and unequivocally. He goes so far as to warn his reader:

> Muhammad says,
> "Love of one's country
> Is part of the faith."
> But don't take that literally!
> Your real "country" is where you're heading,[225]
> Not where you are.
> Don't misread that *hadith*.

(Mesnevi IV, 2210 ff)

Nor is he alone in the realization and the openness that results from the realization; others, both within and beyond the Sufi tradition have acceded to this same truth, from Ibn al-'Arabi to Saint Francis of Assisi to the Ba'al Shem Tov, founder of the Hassidic movement within Jewish mysticism. It is also therefore not surprising that Fethullah Gülen should be among those who have arrived to the same sort of spiritual location.

Gülen recognizes the universalism that defined Rumi, writing that

> [h]e was and continues to be one who beckons, one whose powerful voice invited everyone to the truth and the ultimate blessed reality. Rumi was an inclusive master whose joy was a direct consequence of His [God's] joy, whose love and passion were the result of His [God's] special favors to Rumi... His heart was full of the Divine Light.... His inner eyes were enlightened by this special light.[226]

---

[224] "Reaching" is itself paradoxical, for even reached, the *mysterion* in its most inconceivably absolute innermost hiddenness is never absolutely reached; there remains always a veil, however infinitesimally thin between the mystic and God's *mysterion*—between the seeker and the sought, the lover [mystic] who *succeeds* because s/he is also the sought/beloved and because the beloved [God] is also the seeker/lover.

[225] i.e., heaven: the *sacer*, the *mysterion* of which is the current goal of the mystic and the positive side of which is the hoped for destination of everyone after death.

[226] M. Fethullah Gülen: "Foreword," in Shefik Can, *Fundamentals*, X. We have come full circle back to the closing quotation from Rumi in the preface to this volume and its allusion to the inner eye.

Rumi is part of the continuum of Sufi thinkers, from Rabia' and her emphasis on love; to 'Attar whom Rumi is said to have met when still an adolescent in his father's retinue—who according to the tradition, recognized the young man's gift, and gave him a volume of his ('Attar's) poetry that he kept always by his side—and who is referred to in Rumi's own poetry, along with Sana'i as a beginning point for that poetry;[227] to Ibn al-'Arabi whom young Rumi may well have met in Damascus, as Gülen himself (among others) suggests.[228] Rumi is also a source of key divergences from that continuum. This divergence comes most obviously in Rumi's new and different mode of *dhikr*.

Gülen, too, as much as he may be seen to have a profound connection to Rumi and to have been influenced by Rumi's thinking from a number of different angles—from universal love and compassion to feeling the Presence of God throughout His creation—may also be seen to have drawn sustenance from other Sufis. The doctrine of love that Rabi'a preached and that Rumi expanded into a universalist embrace is central to Gülen's thought. The extension of that *mahabba* outward in all directions to encompass all of nature, because of the conviction that the manifestations of God are found throughout nature and not only throughout humankind—the perspective that Rumi himself in part inherited from Ibn al-'Arabi—may be understood to have been absorbed by Gülen not only from Rumi but from Ibn al-'Arabi himself—albeit turned at a different angle, as we have seen (above, chapter four, 72–3).

To state this last issue otherwise: Rumi's universalist embrace has a starting point, as we have seen, with Ibn al-'Arabi, which exerted influence on Gülen as well as—both directly and through Rumi. The extended discussion and delineation of the path to *fana'* and its spiritual concomitants through a series of *maqamat* and *ahwal* by both al-Qushairi and al-Ghazali, aside from offering a lens through which to focus on leading from thoughts and words to actions may be seen to have helped suggest a systematic *structure* through which theoretical *logoi* can yield the practical *erga* (the sort demanded by Plato's Socrates)

---

[227] Rumi writes: 'Attar was the soul and Sana'i the eyes; I cam after 'Attar and Sana'i...

[228] Gülen writes how Rumi, staying "some time in Damascus,...met many pious persons, such as Ibn al-'Arabi," in his foreword to Shefik Can's *Fundamentals*, xiv.

toward enabling the mystic to achieve intimacy with the *mysterion*. Even more than Rumi, Gülen's absorption of that process has translated *logoi* into *erga* in the specific form of *hizmet*.

Yet ultimately it is Rumi's poetic output that offers the most succinct summary of these issues that have so fully inspired Gülen. And like Rumi, Gülen is both an Islamist and a universalist. As a fervent Muslim, Gülen sees within the Turkey of the past a soul deeply informed by its Muslim identity and the best of the values put forth by Muhammad, the *rashidun* and early caliphs, the Qur'an and the hadith as he has studied and expounded and interpreted them over the many decades of his love affair with his tradition. At the same time he is a universalist in the mold shaped by Rumi, embracing the world: there is paradox but not contradiction to his vision of a Turkey defined by both a Muslim and a universalist identity.

He embraces the Sufi tradition and defines it in self-effacing and altruistic, as well as both universalist and strongly activist, *hizmet*-inducing, terms:

> Sufism has been defined in many ways. Some see it as God's annihilating the individual's ego, will, and self-centeredness and then reviving him or her spiritually with the lights of His Essence. Such a transformation results in God's directing the individual's will in accordance with His Will. Others view it as a continuous striving to cleanse one's self of all that is bad or evil in order to acquire virtue.[229]
>
> Sufism requires the strict observance of all religious obligations, an austere lifestyle, and the renunciation of carnal desires. Through this method of spiritual self-discipline, the individual's heart is purified and his or her senses and faculties are employed in the way of God, which means that the traveler can now begin to live on a spiritual level.[230]

Gülen, whose own lifestyle has consistently reflected this last dictum, arrives at this view not only as a contemporary projection of Rumi, as we have seen, but because he brings two other elements to his teach-

---

[229] "Sufism and Its Origins," in Section Four ("Sufism and Metaphysics") of *Love and Tolerance*, 265.

[230] Ibid, 267.

ings and writings. One is that he is also a student not only of the Sufi tradition that preceded and follows Rumi, from Rabi'a and al-Ghazali (and others) to his contemporary Bediüzzaman Said Nursi; but also from important thinkers beyond that tradition, from Socrates and Plato to Spinoza and Albert Einstein. From each and every one of these thinkers, to repeat, he draws inspiration and an array of important ideas.

But the second element that he brings, as all great thinkers do, is himself: the tapestry that he weaves doesn't simply use the threads of other prior thinkers into a new synthesis. He has his own threads. Love, compassion, tolerance are threads we find him finding in these sources, but expanding on them. We find him furthering the exploration of the ramifications of these ideas that he uses to tie the Muslim tradition to the world at large—not only of other human traditions, but of the elements across the globe and throughout the universe that, beyond the human realm, fall under the umbrella of God-intended human responsibility. Our vice-regency role makes us loving and compassionate caretakers of it all.

His focus on the importance of science but on the equally important application of spiritually-founded principles of how to use science for universal benefit and not personal and ultimately disaster-producing gain may follow a line of thinking articulated earlier by Einstein, but Gülen carries that line further and further within the specific discussions in which he engages as to how to activate these principles.

Activation—*ergon*—may have as a starting point Socrates and Plato, but they could only theorize and would have envied the way in which Gülen has inspired an ever-expanding world of schools and communications outlets to both fulfill the principle of *hizmet* and to spread the word in ever-expanding concentric circles: that the future for Islam and the future of humanity and the future of the planet are one and the same.[231]

---

[231] Plato's single actualized attempt to shape a true *über*-guardian—a philosopher-king—in Dion of Syracuse was a dismal failure that drove Plato back to the refuge of his ivory tower.

Dialogues found in and leading toward love, compassion and tolerance among diverse groups representing diverse faiths, nations and ethnicities and furthering the fundamental idea that we fulfill the Divine Will for us when we serve each other—that serving each other is serving God, even for those who aren't certain that they believe in God— is the starting point with which Gülen expands beyond where Socrates and Plato explicitly sought to carry dialogue.

Gülen's life's work has been no less than an extended expounding upon the words for which Rumi is perhaps best known:

> Come, come wherever you are.
> Wanderer, worshipper, lover of leaving, it doesn't matter…

> "Come, come and join us, as we are the people of love devoted to God! Come, come through the door of love and join us and sit with us. Come, let us speak one to another through our hearts. Let us speak secretly, without ears and eyes. Let us laugh together without lips or sound, let us laugh like the roses. Like thought, let us see each other without any words or sounds. Since all are the same, let us call each other from our hearts, we won't use our lips or tongue. As our hands are clasped together, let us talk about it.[232]

Or from words that, one way or another, Rumi continuously repeated: "…become the light." That is also Gülen's message in three words to those who would follow the lead that he offers in his teachings and his own life.

> In the end, he promises that, as we come to fully recognize that
> Goodness, beauty, truthfulness and being virtuous lie in the essence
> of the world.

then

> [w]hatever happens, the world will one day find this essence, and no one will be able to prevent that [the shining of the light; the leading of the world toward perfection] from happening.[233]

---

[232] From the Rumi quote in Gülen's essay "Love for Humankind," in Section One ("Love and Mercy") of *Love and Tolerance*, 40-1. See above, 88–9.
[233] "Personal Integrity," in *Criteria*, 99.

Bibliography

Aflaki, Shams ad-Din Ahmad, *The Feats of the Knowers of God* (trans. John O'Kane). Leiden: Brill, 2002.

Al-Qushayri. *Principles of Sufism [The Risala]*. (trans. B.R. von Shlegell). Oneonta, NY: Mizan Press, 1990.

Arberry, A.J., *Sufism: An Account of the Mystics of Islam*. New York: Harper Torchbooks, 1970.

Barks, Coleman, with John Moyne, et al, trans., *The Essential Rumi*. San Francisco: HarperColins, 1995.

Can, Shefik. *Fundamentals of Rumi's Thought: A Mevlevi Sufi Perspective*. Somerset, NJ: Tughra Books, 2008.

Carroll, B. Jill, *A Dialogue of Civilizations: Gülen's Islamic Ideals and Humanistic Discourse*. Somerset, NJ: The Light, 2007.

Chittick, William C., *Me and Rumi: The Autobiography of Shams-i Tabrizi*. Louisville, KY: Fons Vitae, 2004.

_____, *The Sufi Path of Knowledge: Ibn al-'Arabi's Metaphysics of Imagination*. Albany: State University of New York Press, 1989.

Ebaugh, Helen Rose. *The Gülen Movement: A Sociological Analysis of a Civic Movement Rooted in Moderate Islam*. Dordrecht: Spring Pub. 2010.

Fadiman, James and Robert Frager, eds., *Essential Sufism*. New York: Harper Collins, 1997.

Fakhry, Majid. *A History of Islamic Philosophy*. NYC: Columbia University Press, 1983.

Gamardi, Ibrahim, *Rumi and Islam*. Woodstock, VT: Skylight Paths, 2004.

Goodman, Lenn E., *Islamic Humanism*. Oxford: Oxford University Press, 2003.

Gülen, M. Fethullah, *Criteria or the Lights of the Way*. London: Truestar Ltd., 1996.

_____, *Essays—Perspectives—Opinions* (Second Edition). Somerset, NJ: The Light, Inc., 2004.

_____, *Key Concepts in the Practice of Sufism: Emerald Hills of the Heart* Somerset, NJ: The Light, 2006. (Reprint of 1996 English-language edition).

_____, *Pearls of Wisdom*. Fairfax, VA: The Fountain, 2000.

_____, *Prophet Muhammad: The Infinite Light*. Izmir: Kaynak, 1998.

_____, *Questions and Answers about Faith*. Fairfax, VA: The Fountain, 2000.

_____, *The Statue of Our Souls: Revival in Islamic Thought and Activism*. Somerset, NJ: The Light, 2005.

_____, *Toward a Global Civilization of Love and Tolerance* (Second Edition). Somerset, NJ: The Light, Inc., 2006.

_____, *Towards the Lost Paradise*. Izmir: Kaynak, 1998.

Ibn al-'Arabi, *The Bezels of Wisdom*. Mahwah, NJ: Paulist Press, 1980.

_____, *The Treatise on Being*, W.H. Weir, transl. London: Beshara Publications, 1975.

Idel, Moshe, *The Mystical Experience in Abraham Abulafia*. Albany: State University of New York Press, 1988.

Kim, Heon and John Raines (eds.), *Making Peace In and With the World: The Role of the Gülen Movement in Eco-Justice*. Newcastle UK: Cambridge Scholars Publishing, 2012.

Lewis, Franklin D., *Rumi: Past and Present, East and West*. Oxford: One World, 2001.

Nicholson, Reynold A., *The Mystics of Islam*. Bloomington, IN: World Wisdom Publications, 2002. (A reprint of the 1914 classic).

Nursi, Bediüzzaman Said, *Ramadan, Frugality, Thanksgiving: from the Risale-i Nur Collection*. Somerset, NJ: The Light, Inc., 2004.

_____, *The Words* (*Sözler*). Istanbul: Sözler Neşriyat, 1998.

Schimmel, Annemarie, *I Am Wind, You Are Fire: The Life and Work of Rumi*. 1992.

Sells, Michael Anthony, *Early Islamic Mysticism*. NJ: Paulist Press, 1995.

Soltes, Ori Z., *Mysticism in Judaism, Christianity and Islam: Searching for Oneness*. Lanham, MD: Rowman & Littlefield Publishers, Inc, 2008.

_____, and Margaret Johnson, eds., *Preventing Violence and Achieving World Peace: Contributions of the Gulen Movement*. New York, NY: Peter Lang Publishers, 2012.

Unal, Ali & Alphonse Williams, compilers, *Fethullah Gülen: Advocate of Dialogue*. Fairfax, VA: The Fountain, 2000.

Vahide, Sukran, *Islam in Modern Turkey: An Intellectual Biography of Bediüzzaman Said Nursi*. Albany: State University of New York Press, 2005.

Valad, Baha ad-Din Muhammad Sultan. *Ibtidaname*. Konya: Konya Turizm Dernegi, 1976.

Van de Weyer, Robert, ed., *Rumi*. London: Hodder & Stoughton, 1998.